Scrapbooking *your* Wedding

fresh ideas for stunning pages

MEMORY
MAKERS
BOOKS

Executive Editor Kerry Arquette   *Founder* Michele Gerbrandt

Art Director Andrea Zocchi

Designer Nick Nyffeler

Production Designer Robin Rozum

Art Acquisitions Editor Janetta Abucejo Wieneke

Craft Editor Jodi Amidei

Photographer Ken Trujillo

Contributing Photographers Brenda Martinez, Terry Ownby, Jennifer Reeves

Cover Photo Stylist Sylvie Abecassis

Contributing Writer Nicole Cummings

Editorial Support Karen Cain, Emily Curry Hitchingman, MaryJo Regier, Lydia Rueger, Dena Twinem

Contributing Memory Makers Masters Joanna Bolick, Jennifer Bourgeault, Kathy Fesmire, Diana Graham,
Diana Hudson, Torrey Miller, Kelli Noto, Michelle Pesce, Trudy Sigurdson, Denise Tucker, Andrea Lyn Vetten-Marley,
Sharon Whitehead, Holle Wiktorek

Memory Makers® *Scrapbooking Your Wedding*
Copyright © 2004 Memory Makers Books

Published by Memory Makers Books, an imprint of F+W Publications, Inc.
12365 Huron Street, Suite 500, Denver, CO 80234
Phone 1-800-254-9124
First edition. Printed in USA.

08 07 06 05 04 5 4 3 2 1

Library of Congress Cataloging-in-Publication Data

Scrapbooking your wedding : fresh ideas for stunning pages / Memory Makers.-- 1st ed.
    p. cm.
    Includes bibliographical references and index.
    ISBN 1-892127-46-6
    1. Photograph albums. 2. Photographs--Conversation and restoration. 3. Scrapbooks. 4.
Weddings. I. Memory Makers Books.

TR465.S397 2004
745.594'1--dc22

                                                                            2004053891

Distributed to trade and art markets by
F+W Publications, Inc.
4700 East Galbraith Road, Cincinnati, OH 45236
Phone 1-800-289-0963

ISBN 1-892127-46-6

Memory Makers Books is the home of *Memory Makers*, the scrapbook magazine dedicated to educating and inspiring scrapbookers.
To subscribe, or for more information, call 1-800-366-6465.
Visit us on the Internet at www.memorymakersmagazine.com

This book belongs to

_____

This book is dedicated to Love.

Table of Contents

Will You Marry Me? 14

Once upon a time there was a little girl who dreamed of a fairy book wedding. She imagined shopping the Kingdom for the most beautiful princess gown to wear and the way her prince would look, dashing and bold, in his tux. There would be celebrations paving the way to the wedding day. Like most good princesses, she would capture all the excitement in photos to create memorable scrapbook pages recording moments from the first "Will you marry me?" to the morning her life would change forever.

- Shopping for the Dress and shoes (16-19)

- Wedding shower and stag party celebrations (20-21)

- Getting primped and perfect (22-25)

We Are Gathered Here Today 26

The carriage pulls up to the chapel and it is like walking into a dream. Flowers bloom from wreaths and vases, filling the air with their perfume. From somewhere inside, programs rustle and hushed voices whisper. And then the Wedding March begins, summoning the procession that leads the way for the bride and groom. The doors in the back of the chapel swing open and breaths are held as the bride and groom enter. The journey that started months earlier moves forward with a sway of silk and satin and the gleam of polished shoes.

- We are gathered here today...: Scrapbooking the chapel (26-29)

- To join this man...: Scrapbooking groom photos (30-35)

- And this woman...: Scrapbooking bride photos (36-45)

- In holy matrimony...: Scrapbooking photos of united hands (46-49)

- In the presence of family and friends...: Scrapbooking photos of the wedding party and guests (50-61)

- Do you take this person...: Scrapbooking photos of the ceremony (62-69)

- I now pronounce you husband and wife...: Scrapbooking first photos of the bride and groom (70-77)

- You may kiss the bride...: Scrapbooking photos of the kiss (78-87)

- I'd like to present Mr. and Mrs....: Scrapbooking formal portraits of the bride and groom (88-101)

- Join us for a celebration! : Scrapbooking photos of the reception including the toast, cake-cutting and first dance (102-113)

And They Lived Happily Ever After 115

And so the story, dreamed once upon a time by a romantic little girl, wove its way from the discovery of a gown to a fairy tale wedding as she and her handsome husband ended the day under a shower of tossed rice. But this was far from The End. It was truly

The Beginning.

Memorabilia 116

Weddings are filled with emotional and romantic mementos including those "old," "new" and "blue" items which the bride wears. There are also invitations, checklists, congratulations cards and much more. Preserve and display these special reminders of a special day on album pages you'll want to look at again and again.

Dreams come True

Our wedding day truly was a dream come true and as I should have known, would be a prediction of what our life together would be like - a wild adventure. Life is continually exciting and challenging. With God as the center of our relationship, together we feel like we can accomplish anything. We make a great team.

Letter of Introduction

Once upon a time I dreamed of finding my own handsome prince. That dream came true when I met Ron Gerbrandt 17 years ago. I knew shortly after meeting him that he was The One. After a short courtship, he asked me to marry him, and of course I said, "yes." The days and weeks that followed were a whirlwind of building excitement that culminated in a celebration of love and dedication. Our wedding will always remain one of my most important and beautiful memories.

If you are a bride-to-be, you are most likely seeking out the best photographer you can find to ensure that your wedding activities are recorded in splendid photos. If you are a newly-wed, you are reliving the fanfare of your pre-wedding celebrations and the uniqueness of the ceremony by reviewing the photos that document these happy times. Wedding photos never grow less precious as the years turn over. In fact, those of us who have been married for decades still find ourselves reliving the excitement of our wedding through our pictures.

This book, *Scrapbooking Your Wedding*, is intended to help brides, grooms and those who are scrapbooking wedding photos for friends and family members create scrapbook pages that are as beautiful as the Sacred Event. You'll find more than 100 scrapbook pages designed to inspire you and cutting-edge techniques that are illustrated in step-by-step photos, making it possible for you to re-create them on your own. *Scrapbooking Your Wedding* includes a special look at a wedding theme album which may help you create your own cohesive wedding scrapbook, as well as memorabilia and photo checklists. An additional chapter features scrapbook pages that offer ideas for including memorabilia in your album.

I'd like to thank the brides and grooms who shared a piece of their special day with us by allowing Memory Makers to publish their photos and pages. I would also like to thank the dozens of scrapbook artists and photographers whose work graces the pages of this book. *Scrapbooking Your Wedding* honors all of these contributors—it also honors Love, which is one of the greatest blessings of all.

May your life be filled with joy and may these happy events be recorded on beautiful scrapbook pages that celebrate your personal Once Upon a Time love story's Happy Ending.

Best,

Michele

Michele Gerbrandt
Founder, Memory Makers

Basic Scrapbook Tools and Supplies

Every artist, from cinematographer to sculptor, painter to musician needs the right tools and supplies in order to create. Scrapbook artists are no exception. Before you begin scrapbooking your wedding photos, take a trip to your local scrapbook or craft store, or visit one of the many suppliers of scrapbook supplies online. You'll want to stock up on the basics and a wealth of wonderful materials that will result in simply stunning scrapbook pages.

Adhesives

Modern scrapbook adhesives ensure strong binding of photos, memorabilia and embellishments to scrapbook papers without damaging photos or memorabilia. They are available in a variety of forms including glue pens and sticks, photo splits and tape runners. Some varieties offer permanent bonding and others allow you to remove your photos at a later date.

Stickers, Stamps and Templates

Available in countless designs and patterns that suit almost every page theme, these tools are used to add decorative designs and shapes to your scrapbook pages. Emboss over their design, color within their borders, use them as guidelines for journaling. The opportunities are endless.

Embellishments

Tags, beads, fibers, charms and other adornments are used to decorate and add flair to scrapbook pages. Combine them or use them alone for customized decorating.

Pens and Markers

From fine-point to large brush styles, these tools are used in journaling as well as for adding decorative flourishes to page design. Choose writing tools that are safe for scrapbooking. Practice using your writing tool on scrap paper before attempting to write directly on your scrapbook page.

Albums

Albums are sold in a variety of styles including post-bound, strap-hinge, three-ring binder and spiral as well as a variety of sizes from 4 x 6" to 12 x 15". Choose one that best suits your shelf space and works well with your personal scrapbooking style.

Cutting Tools

Decorative scissors, paper trimmers, craft knives, punches and shape cutters are used to create decorative mats, journaling and title blocks as well as crop photos and create decorative page elements. Whether cutting straight edges, curving corners or creating whimsical shapes, there is a cutting tool for every job.

Paper

Paper is available in solid cardstock and in hundreds of festive and artistic patterns and also as specialty papers including vellum, suede, mulberry, handmade paper and metallics. Paper is used for backgrounds, matting, page elements such as journaling blocks and borders as well as design additions.

Create a Layout

The scrapbook page is your canvas. Your wedding photos, journaling and embellishments are the elements you use to create your masterpiece. There are no hard-and-fast rules when it comes to the creation of a scrapbook page, however many strong layouts build on common themes and design principles.

Focal Point

Choose an enlarged, matted, unique or exceptional photo for your page's primary focal point. The goal is not only to capture the viewer's attention, but also to visually ground your layout. All surrounding photos should support this central image.

Balance

Place your photos on one- or two-page layouts. Note that very large, bright or busy photos may dominate the page and need to be balanced by less-busy counterparts. Move the photos around until you've achieved a look that is visually appealing. Remember to leave space for a page title, journaling and embellishments.

Color

Choose a background, mat papers and design additions that complement your photos. Consider pulling colors found in the pictures themselves, or select colors that help reinforce your page theme. When it comes to color, less is often more, so be selective in your choices and don't let the colors on the page overwhelm the photos.

Crop and Assemble

Cropping

Photo cropping can remove a busy background from a picture or reduce the image to a workable size or more interesting shape. Never crop one-of-a-kind photos. Work on duplicates.

Matting

Photo mats provide an island for your pictures which grounds them and draws the viewer's eye, adding visual balance and contrast. Photo mats serve as a buffer between memorabilia that is potentially damaging and pictures. Photo mats can be cut in decorative shapes, can be layered or embellished.

Mounting

Photos, memorabilia, journaling and title blocks are mounted on scrapbook pages with archivally safe adhesives. You may also wish to use photo corners to mount your materials. These corners are adhered to the background paper of a page and the corners of photo mats are inserted, allowing the photos to be removed at a later date, if desired.

Title and Journaling

A creative title announces the theme of your scrapbook page, and journaling is a way of recording the details surrounding the page. Journaling often cites the date the photos were taken, those appearing in the pictures and information about the event. It may be done as bullets, quotes, sayings, poems or a personal reflection. Write directly on your scrapbook page or create title or journaling blocks and mount them in your album.

Embellish

Much of the fun in the creation of a scrapbook layout is in the embellishing. Whether you wish to decorate your page with ribbon, fiber or punched paper shapes, stickers, beads, charms, tiny metal frames or other ephemera, you'll find that dressing up your page provides the finishing touch.

The Completed Page

The completed page brings together all your elements in an artistic and emotional display of images and words. It tells a story about a person or an event in a way that you and your descendants will be able to relate to in decades to come. It is testimony to your talent and to your caring.

Creating a Wedding Theme Album

A wedding album should be as beautiful as the wedding itself. Unlike other albums, theme albums focus on a single topic such as a family's Christmas celebrations, vacations or, of course, a WEDDING! A successful theme album reads like a well-designed book with obvious flow between the pages.

Color in a theme album is consistent throughout the book. Choose a few colors that work well together and with the photos you will be showcasing. Look for clues in the bride's flowers, the bridesmaid dresses or the surrounding landscape.

A title page is an asset to a theme album because it heralds the pages to come. Consider using a poem, song lyric or special quote on your title page to establish the mood and intention of your album.

All art featured on pages 12-13 by Lori Dickhaut, Sherwood Park, Alberta, Canada

Photos in a well-designed theme album are visually supportive of one another and tell the story from beginning to end. Seek continuity in style and lighting.

Photo List

In the bustle of wedding activities you could easily forget to take photos of important events. Use this checklist to ascertain that you take photos of:

Shopping for the dress
Shopping for the tux
Shopping for the cake and flowers
Shopping for thank-you gifts for wedding
party members
Scouting trips to churches and restaurants
Bridal shower and stag party
Salon visits to prepare hair and nails
Behind-the-scenes preparations
Bride and groom preparations
Bride and flower girl

Groom and ring bearer
Bride and bridesmaids
Bride and parents
Bride and siblings
Bride alone
Groom and groomsmen
Groom and parents
Groom and siblings
Groom alone
Church exterior
Arrival of bride and groom at church
Processional
Father's goodbye kiss
Musicians
Minister, rabbi or pastor
Candle lighting

Special traditions
Exchange of vows
Bride and groom kiss
Recessional
Rice throwing or other send-off celebration
Bridal party and other formal portraits
First dance and dancing guests
The toast
The cake and cake-cutting
The rings
Bouquet/garter toss
Gifts
Signature book
The marriage certificate
Cards
Table decorations

Spreads, rather than single pages, are the backbone of a theme album. When laying out your photos, consider the balance between two pages that, when viewed, will be seen as one. Design your spreads so that larger focal photos will be supported on the opposite page by smaller photos and memorabilia.

Embellishments are an important part of any album and especially so in a theme album. These decorative elements pull together the colors utilized throughout the book and carry the intent of the story. Keep them minimal and look for variations on the technique that can be modified in order to maintain interest through the album.

Memorabilia Checklist

Preparation notes
Bulletins
Invitations
Guest list
Guest signatures
Handwritten vows
Sheet music
Bridal bouquet
Garter
Pressed flowers
Napkins
Confetti/rice
Favors
Marriage license
Receipts
Business cards of florist, caterers
Copy of gift registry
Congratulations cards

Text in a theme album is consistent in type, style and size. While a theme album may use a select number of diverse fonts, they should be compatible—no blocky fonts mixed arbitrarily with flowing scripts. Choose a type style that suits the general mood of the album.

Will You...

Marry me?

Once upon a time
there was a LOVE story that began
with *"How do you do?"* and wove its way to

"Will you marry me?"

Yes

And then there was shopping, celebrations
and preparations. And the
air rang with laughter
and *giddy expectation.*

Creating the Perfect Dress

A perfect dress, created by a grandmother, forms the theme for this perfect page. Begin with two patterned paper backgrounds. Mat photos on decoratively cropped cream textured cardstock blocks and brown patterned paper; stitch around edge of brown mat and mount photos. Print journaling and "beautiful" definition on cream textured cardstock; print title and photo captions on brown patterned paper. Cut title into pieces and mat on decorative-cropped cream textured cardstock mats. Use eyelets to mount title portions and photo captions; add fabric swatch and dress sticker.

Allyson Ell, Victoria, British Columbia, Canada

Supplies: Patterned paper background (Creative Imaginations); cream textured cardstock (Bazzill); brown patterned paper (source unknown); decorative scissors (Fiskars); dress sticker (EK Success); eyelets; fabric

Remember

A pretty, feminine layout of this tiny flower girl is enhanced with lace and ribbon. Adhere trimmed piece of floral patterned paper on white textured cardstock background and mount doily on top. String sheet ribbon through eyelets set in corners of patterned paper piece to create frame. Mat focal photo on torn white textured cardstock; mount. Crop remaining photos; mat and mount. Journal on transparency; mount with clear photo corners. Apply rub-on word to photo; embellish with satin bow. Wrap corners of page with tulle and adorn with paper flowers.

Heather Melzer, Yorkville, Illinois

Supplies: Floral patterned paper and white textured card-stock (Chatterbox): rub-on word (Making Memories); eyelets; sheet ribbon; doily; transparency; ribbon; tulle; paper flowers

The Brown Dress

Begin by cutting windows in foam core board for title and row of photos across the page's bottom. Cut dark green cardstock to cover foam core, leaving window openings free. Adhere light green cardstock over dark green, leaving room for darker cardstock to show around windows and edges. Adhere patterned paper block to upper right corner. Adhere lace across two strips of light green cardstock cut to fit in title and photo windows. Mount photos to lace and adhere behind foam core window opening. Mount title strip behind window opening. Create title tiles using decorative tiles following the directions below. Print part of title and journaling on transparency; adhere over lace and across window opening. Mount sepia photo. Complete title with letter stickers affixed on inked stone tile to read "the." Attach to page with ribbon and heart brad. Embellish page with green ribbon, pearls, heart brads and inked stone tiles. Apply date with number stickers.

Torrey Miller, Thornton, Colorado

Supplies: Chalk inks (Tsukineko); stone tiles (Clearsnap); letter and number stickers (Creative Imaginations); patterned paper (K & Company); pearl strands (Jo-Ann Fabric); green heart brads (Provo Craft); lace; blue, ivory and green cardstocks; foam core; transparency; green ribbon

1 Colorize stone tiles with chalk ink using finger dauber or other sponge applicator.

2 Apply letter stickers to select chalked tiles to spell "dress" and "The."

The Dress

A special homemade dress is honored on this perfectly stitched page. Trim tan cardstock slightly smaller than white cardstock background. Wrap lace pieces around edges of tan cardstock background. Print journaling on vellum, leaving room for separate torn journaling strips; mount. Affix black ribbon across center, and sheer white ribbon diagonally on page. Crop photos; mat on black cardstock. Print descriptive words "the lace," "the pearls," and "the veil" on torn vellum; adhere on matted photos before mounting. Mat bride photo on black cardstock; wrap top corners with black ribbon and mount. Embellish page corners with lace, buttons, zipper and threaded needle. Sew on alphabet button title. Print remaining journaling on torn vellum; mount and add buttons. Mount tan cardstock piece on white cardstock background.

Debbie Hill for Junkitz, Lansdale, Pennsylvania

Supplies: Self-adhesive zipper, decorative buttons, alphabet buttons (Junkitz); tan, white and black cardstocks; lace; vellum; black and sheer white ribbons; white floss; threaded needle

Father of the Bride

A little girl plays dress-up in Mommy's wedding dress as her father looks on in an emotional bridal page. Tear corner sections from red floral patterned paper and mount on two sheets of ivory textured cardstock. For left page background, manipulate and enlarge photo of father; adhere and cover with vellum. Print title on torn ivory textured cardstock and mount. Mat smaller photos on red floral paper and double mat large father photo on ivory textured cardstock and red floral paper; mount. Mount sepia bridal photo. For right page, adhere remaining photos, layering and matting with ivory textured cardstock and red floral paper. Adhere vellum section across portion of the page. Journal on torn ivory textured cardstock; mount. Stamp phrases on vellum. Line up on both pages and adhere. Embellish with buttons.

Ginger McSwain, Cary, North Carolina

Supplies: Ivory textured cardstock (DMD); red floral patterned paper, buttons (EK Success); letter stamps (PSX Design); vellum; floss; black ink

A Dream and a Vision

Black-and-white photos help to create a page with color-ful emotion. Adhere section of silver mesh vertically on black cardstock background. Mount section of patterned paper horizontally across net and background at bottom of page; mount photos. Print poem on torn white textured cardstock; mount with "dream" label. Embellish tag with heart charm and mount.

Julie Phelan, Quincy, Illinois

Supplies: Silver mesh (Making Memories); patterned papers (7 Gypsies); textured cardstock (Southworth); label maker (Dymo); heart charm (Boutique Trims); tag; black cardstock

The Bride and Her Daughter

Just the right dress can turn big and little girls into princesses, as witnessed on this stylish page. Affix border sticker across center of patterned paper background. Mat "bride" photos on cream cardstock; attach decorative photo corners and mount. Cut eight rectangular blocks from floral patterned paper; ink edges and mount four pieces in each of the top right and lower left page corners. Mat letter stickers on inked cardstock pieces and adhere on floral sections in top right corner; embellish with heart-shaped lace. Decorate lower left corner with large tag embellished with pearls, stamped words, ribbon, stickers and tiny dress. Journal on vellum; mount on page along with remaining photo embellished with decorative photo corner stickers.

Mary Bautista Marty, Chula Vista, California

Supplies: Border sticker, patterned paper, letter stickers, stamp (Anna Griffin); decorative photo corners (Boutique Trims); floral patterned paper, word sticker (Daisy Hill); letter stickers and dress sticker (EK Success); letter stamps (PSX Design); word ribbon, swirl clips (Making Memories); decorative photo corner stickers (K & Company); cream cardstock; black ink; lace embellishment; large and tiny tags; pearl strand; ribbon; vellum

Celebrate

A great bridal shower is commemorated on an equally great page. Mount torn section from floral patterned paper at bottom of sanded purple linen paper background. Mat photos with purple and black cardstocks and striped patterned paper. Cover smaller photos with die-cut frame; tie black ribbon around one photo before mounting all. Journal on torn and chalked white cardstock. Mat journaling block on black cardstock and mount. Embellish photos and bridal shower invitation with handcut paper flowers. Stamp title and mount on black cardstock strip; mount on page. Stamp additional journaling on torn purple paper strips; attach to page and invitation. Mat embellished invitation on black cardstock and mount.

Holle Wiktorek, Reunion, Colorado

Supplies: Floral, purple linen and striped patterned papers, die-cut frame (Chatterbox); bridal shower invitation (Razzle Dazzle); letter stamps (PSX Design, La Pluma); sandpaper; purple, black and white cardstocks; sheer black ribbon; purple and charcoal chalks; black and white inks; purple brads

Bridal Shower

Special moments during a bridal shower are featured in the photos on this party page. Sand edges of circles cut from patterned papers. Mount on green textured cardstock background, hanging larger circle off right edge and trimming away excess. Embellish pink paper title block with pink textured cardstock strip and button. Create "Bridal" portion of title with green vellum letter stickers. Print remaining portion of title on ivory cardstock; cut out leaving edge for faux mat and mount. Mount sanded plaid patterned paper strip across top of page. Cut two sections of pink paper; sand and ink edges. Crop photos and white cardstock into squares; adhere on sections of pink paper. Label photos with word stickers, letter stickers and a tag. Embellish white squares with buttons and gift stickers. Print place and date on strip of pink textured cardstock; adhere patterned paper strip and button and mount across bottom of page.

Jennifer Bourgeault, Macomb Township, Michigan

Supplies: Patterned papers, word stickers, letter stickers, tag (Chatterbox); green and pink textured cardstocks (Bazzill); vellum letter stickers (Mrs. Grossman's); gift stickers (EK Success); pink buttons; green floss; sandpaper; green ink; white cardstock; pink brads

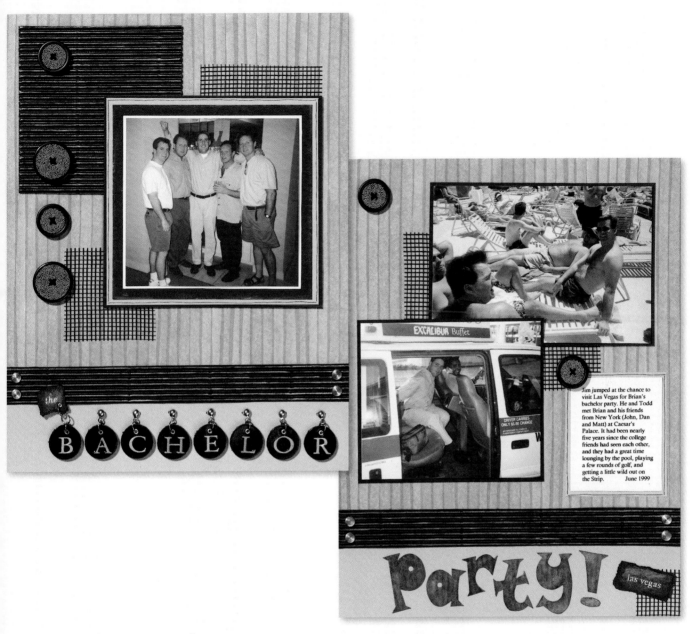

The journaling block reads:

Jim jumped at the chance to visit Las Vegas for Brian's bachelor party. He and Todd met Brian and his friends from New York (John, Dan and Matt) at Caesar's Palace. It had been nearly five years since the college friends had seen each other, and they had a great time lounging by the pool, playing a few rounds of golf, and getting a little wild out on the Strip.   June 1999

Bachelor Party

A celebration is captured in full-throttle on this strongly presented spread. Begin by adhering a strip of light green paper onto the bottom of a sheet of patterned paper. Cut strips and a square of corrugated black cardstock and treat with metallic rub-ons. Adhere strip to bottom of pages and secure with nailheads. Mount treated block at upper left corner of left page. Mount sections of mesh to both pages; mount matted photos and journaling block atop mesh sections. Adhere micro bead to center of stitched buttons and mount on page. For first part of title, attach leather alphabet disks with jump rings and brads to left page. Use template for "Party!" title portion and treat with metallic rub-ons; mount on right page.

Stacy Hackett, Murrieta, California

Supplies: Patterned paper (Mustard Moon); corrugated paper (DMD); rub-ons (Making Memories); leather letters (EK Success); lettering template (Scrap Pagerz); mesh; metallic rub-ons; jump rings; nailheads; buttons; adhesive; floss

A Single Moment

A groom's wedding-day thoughts are nicely displayed on this masculine layout. Print title directly onto white textured cardstock background. Scan and print paisley pattern from groom's vest. Layer section of paisley-printed photo with sections of black cardstock and black velvet paper on left side of page. Triple mat photo on black cardstock and paisley photo paper, embellish photo and mat with two black photo corners. Mount photo on page along with smaller matted photo. Journal on vellum block; add photo corner and mount. Embellish with ribboned red velvet leaves and straight pin.

Elizabeth Ruuska, Rensselaer, Indiana

Supplies: White textured cardstock (Bazzill); black velvet paper (Paper Adventures); black photo corners (Fiskars); black cardstock; vellum; velvet ribbon; velvet leaves; stick pin

A Single Moment

He spends the last few moments before the ceremony alone. He realizes this is the last time he will be alone. In a few moments he will no longer be single. He will be married, a husband to his best friend. Even when they are apart, he will never be truly alone. He realizes this in a single moment—the last of his single moments.

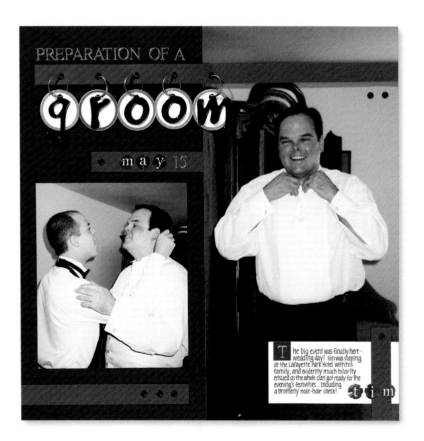

Preparation of a Groom

The groom is all gussied up on this dressy-but-masculine groom page. Adhere enlarged photo on right side of black cardstock background; set black eyelets in corner. Journal on white cardstock leaving out the first letter of first word; adhere on photo with burgundy cardstock strip, letter stickers and eyelet. Replace missing letter with letter sticker matted on black cardstock. Cover die-cut letters in lacquer; mount on metal-rimmed tags and hang from eyelets set in burgundy cardstock strip. Mount with foam adhesive. Finish title with letter stickers affixed above tags. Mount remaining photo on page. Attach burgundy strips with eyelets; affix letter and number stickers for date.

Michelle Pesce, Arvada, Colorado
Photo: Cheryl Pesce, Trabuco Canyon, California

Supplies: Letter stickers (Chatterbox, Pioneer); die-cut letters (Current); crystal lacquer (Ranger); black, white and burgundy cardstocks; metal-rimmed tags; foam adhesive; eyelets

The Path of Friendship

This altered style layout features the special bond between the groom and his brother. Adhere focal photo on left side of patterned paper background. Enhance embossed paper with brown chalk and brown metallic rubs-ons. Tear corner pieces and ink edges; attach to page with brads. Cut swirl piece from extra piece of enhanced embossed paper; mount on photo. Stamp title on page. Sand and ink edges of smaller photo; attach brads in corners and mount on page with foam adhesive. Mix solution of 85 percent acrylic paint and 15 percent crystal lacquer; paint all metal page embellishments. Sand metal plaque; mount with decorative brads on page. Create small journaling book by following the directions below.

Colleen Macdonald, Winthrop, Australia
Photos: Kelli Noto, Centennial, Colorado

Supplies: Patterned paper (Paper Loft); embossed paper (K & Company); metallic rub-ons (Craf-T); various letter stamps (Hero Arts, Rubber Stampede, Wordsworth); metal plaques, decorative brads (Making Memories); crystal lacquer (Sakura Hobby Craft); hinges and catches (National Artcraft); brown chalk; brown ink; brads; foam adhesive; sandpaper; acrylic paints; brown cardstock

1 Cut out center of embossed paper for cover of book. Use finger to apply brown metallic rub-ons and chalks to surface of paper to highlight the raised portions of the paper pattern.

2 Cut out pages of small book from brown cardstock enhancing edges with acrylic paint; adhere embossed piece on top.

3 Attach book to background page with hinges, latch and brads.

Ready

This bride is in the pink despite the black-and-white photos that capture her dilemma of managing an updo and unmanageable slip. Mat gray cardstock on black cardstock background. Create scroll designs on gray portion of background with acrylic paint and a stencil. Adhere patterned vellum strip on white cardstock strip; mount. Mount pink patterned paper on bottom half of page and adhere ribbon at seam. Paint metal title word; tie with sheer ribbons and mount. Use photo corners to mat focal photo on patterned paper; mat again on gray and black cardstocks. Mat one remaining photo on pink cardstock; mount all remaining photos. Journal on transparency; mount. Embellish page corner with fabric label. Stamp date on small tag; paint edges, set and embellish eyelet with rhinestone brad. Mount ring.

Diana Graham, Barrington, Illinois
Photos: Crane's Picture Perfect, Lake Zurich, Illinois

Supplies: Scroll stencils (Plaid); patterned vellum, patterned paper (Treehouse Designs); fabric label, metal word, date stamp (Making Memories); pink rhinestone (Magic Scraps); ring embellishment (source unknown); gray, black and white cardstocks; pink acrylic paint; sheer ribbons; photo corners; small tag; eyelet

Getting Ready

Half the fun for this bride was getting ready for the big day, as seen on this upbeat page. Mount section of blue stitched paper on patterned paper background. Adhere twill tape along seam. Single and double mat two photos on blue stitched paper and pink and white cardstocks. Journal on white cardstock block; mat on pink cardstock and mount. Stamp title and phrases on white cardstock; cut out. Tie sheer blue ribbon through holes punched in title; mount. Attach phrases to twill with safety pins tied with sheer blue ribbon. Mount plaque.

Tracy Miller, Fallston, Maryland

Supplies: Patterned paper, plaque (Li'l Davis Designs); blue stitched paper (Jennifer Collection); letter stamps (Ma Vinci's, PSX Design); twill tape; pink and white cardstocks; safety pins; blue ink; sheer blue ribbon

Finishing Touches

Mini glass marbles make photo frames unforgettable on this sparkling wedding page. Layer torn patterned papers on tan cardstock background; chalk edges. Embellish upper corners with lace, ribbon, flower button and pearl strand. Cut frames for photos from floral patterned paper; tear outer edges. Cover frames in paper glaze then mini glass marbles. When dry, embellish corners with lace, ribbon, pearls, buttons and tulle. Mount over photos onto page. Print title on vellum leaving out first letters of each word. Cut missing letters from patterned paper; cover with glaze and mini glass marbles then mount with vellum words on page. Journal on torn and chalked vellum; mount. Cover small and medium tags with patterned papers; embellish and mount.

Jeanne McKinney, Huntersville, North Carolina
Photos: Gregg Owen For Professional Photographic Services, Charlotte, North Carolina

Supplies: Patterned papers (7 Gypsies, Frances Meyer); flower buttons (Jesse James); paper glaze (Duncan); mini glass marbles (Halcraft); lettering template (Provo Craft); page pebble (Making Memories); tan cardstock; chalk; lace; ribbon; pearl strands; vellum; tulle

"I Do" Hairdo

A prolonged trip to the hairdresser resulted in a top-notch "do" on this top-notch page. Mount squares cut from polka-dot patterned paper and black cardstock on ivory textured cardstock background. Print "hair" repeatedly on green cardstock strip; mount at page left. Double mat focal photo on black cardstock and green patterned paper. Mat magazine clipping on black cardstock mat; journal and embellish with circle and bamboo clips and metal label. Mount photos on page; embellish with daisies and label stickers. Journal on green patterned paper; mount. Apply title letter stickers to page and on small square mats. Apply "me" with stickers to cardstock circle and tuck under photo.

Leah Blanco Williams, Kansas City, Missouri
Photo: Christa Hoffarth Photography, Omaha, Nebraska

Supplies: Polka-dot patterned paper (Chatterbox); ivory textured cardstock (Bazzill); green patterned paper (Mustard Moon); bamboo clip (Jest Charming); metal label (DieCuts with a View); daisies (Sarah Heidt Photo Craft); letter stickers (Colorbök, Pioneer, S.R.M. Press); circle clip; label stickers

Getting Ready, Here We Come

This delightful spread showcases the doll-like qualities of two little girls in the wedding party and keeps this spread feeling intimate. Trim patterned paper and mat on black cardstock backgrounds. Mat photos on black cardstock; layer on page over red textured cardstock blocks. Punch tiny leaves from cream textured cardstock strips; mat on black cardstock and mount on red textured cardstock blocks. Apply title letter stickers on cream textured cardstock pieces; mat and mount on pages.

Linda Beeson, Ventura, California

Supplies: Patterned paper (Colorbök); red and cream textured cardstocks (DMD); leaf punch (All Night Media); letter stickers (Me & My Big Ideas); black cardstock

October 15, 1983

First Baptist Church
Galesburg, Illinois

We are gathered here today...

The morning of the ceremony dawns electric with expectation. Inside the cathedral flowers seem to bloom with wild abandon. With hushed voices, the guests await the arrival of the bride and groom. A herald of music joins the heavy perfume of blossoms in the air. The doors swing open and, with a shine of shoes and the rustle of silk, the ceremony begins.

Fairytales Do Come True

The tulle on a bride's dress is reflected on this wedding page in a frothy embellishment. Mat trimmed patterned paper on green cardstock background. Mount white cardstock page corners on corners of patterned paper and adorn with white buttons. Double mat photo on white and green cardstocks and mount. Gather section of tulle at ends and tie with white silk ribbons; mount across bottom of page. Print title in varied fonts on white cardstock; cut out "Fairytales" letters, mat on green cardstock and mount. Crop "do come true" portion of title and mat on green cardstock before mounting.

Erica Campbell, Imperial, Missouri

Supplies: Patterned paper (Amscan); green and white cardstocks; white buttons; tulle; white silk ribbon

Always & Forever

A perspective on a stunning gown along with floral embellishments make this page special. Begin by layering inked sections of green floral and script patterned paper with tan mulberry paper on cardstock background. Adhere black velvet strips strategically across page. Embellish with velvet bows and silk flowers. Affix die-cut title letters on script paper section. Double mat focal photo on black cardstock and inked tan mulberry, single mat smaller photo on black cardstock; mount. Mat tag cut from tan mulberry on black cardstock and top with journaled transparency. Embellish and mount.

Kelli Noto, Centennial, Colorado

Supplies: Green and script patterned papers (Design Originals); chalk ink (Clearsnap); die-cut letters (Quic-Kutz); silk roses (EK Success); tan mulberry paper; black velvet; black cardstock; transparency

Manti

Uniquely painted papers bring a glow to this unusual wedding page. Adhere brown mesh paper on brown cardstock background; mount section of sheer flower embroidered fabric on right side of page. Wrap edges of page in gold crinkle paper to create a frame; sew on. Create painted enhancement paper by following the directions below. Cut two strips from painted enhancement paper and sew onto brown lip cord; mount horizontally across page. Mat torn photo on block of torn painted enhancement paper; mount on lip cord. Journal on torn vellum; mount. Handcut title; mat on brown cardstock. Paint tag gold, set eyelet and string with copper wire. Journal on tag, hang from title and mount title and tag on page; embellish with heart button. Write date on vellum; mount under label holder.

Samantha Walker, Battle Ground, Washington
Photos: Mark Philbrick Photography, Orem, Utah

Supplies: Watercolor paper (Arches); green, yellow and sienna acrylic paints (Windsor Newton Gallery); gold acrylic paint; brown mesh paper and gold crinkle paper (FLAX art & design); sheer embroidered fabric (Reena's Creations); heart button (JBW); brown cardstock; lip cord; vellum; small tag; eyelet; copper wire; label holder

1 Create enhancement paper by sponging green, yellow and sienna acrylic paints onto thick cardstock or watercolor paper, alternating colors. Take care not to overload sponge. Remove excess paint from sponge by blotting on a paper towel.

2 When acrylic paint is dry, sponge on gold paint to finish.

To join this man...

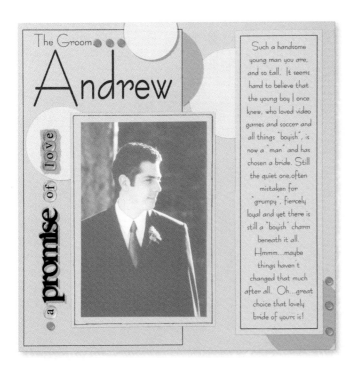

A Promise of Love

Clean lines and concise circles add visual interest to this loving layout. Journal portions of title and vertical phrase on green textured cardstock background; add rectangle frame. Cut circles from light and dark green textured cardstocks; adhere along with brads. Finish title with metal black-inked "promise" word and "love" word printed on darker green cardstock. Mount both vertically on page. Cover select letters with page pebbles. Mat photo on purple textured cardstock; draw frame around mat border. Journal on purple textured cardstock; add frame, print and mount.

Sharon Whitehead, Vernon, British Columbia, Canada

Supplies: Light and dark green and purple textured cardstocks (Bazzill); metal letter, page pebbles (Making Memories); brads; black ink; ruler; pen

The Tux

A handsome masculine layout suits this groom to the "T"-ux. Begin with two black textured cardstock backgrounds. On left page, layer white textured cardstock piece. Double mat photo on black and white cardstocks and mount over white cardstock background. Mount sections of silver paper to background with square brads. Print "Simply Irresistible" on strip of vellum and attach with square brads. Print title on white textured cardstock; mat on torn silver paper block and attach with brads. On right page, single and double mat photos, printing descriptive words on larger mat; mount.

Lori Dickhaut, Sherwood Park, Alberta, Canada

Supplies: Black and white textured cardstocks (Bazzill); silver paper (Paper Adventures); small and large square brads; vellum

The Knight Who Brings Me Camelot

A groom's extraordinary efforts in planning his wedding and finding a new home for his bride is documented on this noble page. Print journaling onto cream cardstock background; adhere cut strips of patterned papers. Mat photos on red, green and black cardstocks; ink edges and mount. Cut select title letters from white cardstock; ink edges and mount with rub-on letters to complete title. Stamp medal image at top of page and cover with vellum quote.

Leah Blanco Williams, Kansas City, Missouri
Photo: Christa Hoffarth Photography, Omaha, Nebraska

Supplies: Patterned papers (Anna Griffin, Carolee's Creations, Chatterbox, Karen Foster Design, Mustard Moon, Rusty Pickle); rub-on letters (Woodland Scenics); medal image (Stampabilities); vellum quote (Memories Complete); cream, red, green and black cardstocks; black ink

The Groom

Ribbons and handmade paper help to offer up a page with beautiful texture. Wrap ribbons around trimmed white mulberry paper, securing; adhere mulberry section on black textured paper background. Adorn frame cut from textured paper with knotted ribbon pieces and mount on page over photo. Rub metal title plate and photo corners with liquid pigment powder; mount and hang tassel. Affix letter stickers on title plate and at bottom of page. Stamp date below photo.

Jeniece Higgins, Lake Forest, Illinois

Supplies: White mulberry and black textured papers (Provo Craft); ribbons, photo corners, date stamp (Making Memories); liquid pigment powder (AMACO); metal plate (Artistic Expressions); letter stickers (Creative Imaginations); tassel

Kiss the Single Life Goodbye

Photos of a funny moment between the groom and grooms-man offer the foundation for a page so upbeat it makes you smile. Adhere torn sections of red and tan patterned papers on black cardstock background. Stitch an "X" pattern along the torn edge of the red patterned paper piece. Apply title with letters cut from template using various patterned papers, epoxy letter stickers and printed and colored words. Mount on page over silver mesh; adorn with silk flowers and decorative buckle. Double and single mat photos on tan patterned paper, red cardstock and corrugated paper. Attach corrugated matted photo onto page with brads; mount remaining photo on page. Journal onto vellum; attach with brads.

Holle Wiktorek, Reunion, Colorado
Photos: Narcissus Magturo of NAM Photography,
Ft. Leonard Wood, Missouri

Supplies: Red patterned paper (source unknown); tan patterned paper (source unknown); patterned paper (Daisy D's); epoxy letter stickers (Li'l Davis Designs); silk flowers (Making Memories); decorative buckle (source unknown); corrugated paper (DMD); silver mesh; black and red cardstocks; gel pens; brads; vellum

Becoming a Husband

A husband is so very special and so is this summer-fresh scrapbook page. Mat green patterned paper on green cardstock background. Print "Becoming A" portion of title on lighter green cardstock before mounting piece on darker section of partially torn cardstock block; mount in upper left page corner. Print descriptive words on green cardstock; tear into strips and layer on top of marbled paper before mounting section onto page corners. Make frame from green cardstock; mount photo. Wrap sheer knotted ribbon around upper corners and across bottom of photo. Print name and date on cardstock; affix on back of label holders tied with ribbon. Wrap ribbons around bottom of page and matted photo. Attach additional ribbon to back of photo mat; string with ribbon charm, knot ends and adhere mat to page. Affix ivy stickers and letter stickers to complete title on upper left corner. Mat "H" on die-cut circles.

Kathy Fesmire, Athens, Tennessee
Photo: Portraits By Cheri Ellis, Cleveland, Tennessee

Supplies: Green patterned paper (Frances Meyer); marbled paper (Karen Foster Design); die-cut circles (Sizzix); ivy and letter stickers (K & Company); label holders, ribbon charm (Making Memories); dark and light green card-stocks; chalk; ribbon

The Groom

A mini handmade photo album adds a special touch to this Prince Charming page. Create the mini album by following the directions below. Make background page from sections of red patterned and linen patterned papers stitched onto black cardstock background. Stitch a black cardstock pocket to bottom right page corner to hold photo album. Stamp journaling on linen paper with letter stamps. Emboss edges of photo with silver embossing powder and mount. Add handcut title.

Samantha Walker, Battle Ground, Washington
Photos: Mark Philbrick Photography, Orem, Utah

Supplies: Linen, smoky and red patterned papers (Chatterbox, FLAX art & design, Wausau Papers); letter stamps (Stampin' Up!); letter stickers, word stickers, black embossed frame (Chatterbox); charm (Making Memories); cardboard; black ink; black and tan cardstocks; glue; silver embossing powder

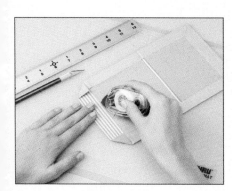

1 To make photo album, wrap and glue linen patterned paper on two same-sized cardboard pieces. Leave small gap between pieces to form binding.

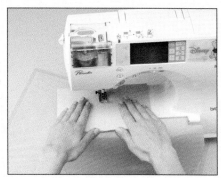

2 Cut papers for inside of book; stitch together down center.

3 Adhere stitched pages to album cover along center seam and front and back pages to inside of cover.

Key To My Heart

A heartfelt groom page is made rich with touching journaling. Journal on patterned vellum, leaving out the first word. Cut into a circular shape and mount on wide strip of green patterned paper; trim excess vellum edges. Mount piece on gold textured paper; line top and bottom edges with black cardstock. Mount photo with black photo corners on inked white cardstock; double mat on black cardstock and mount. Use letter stickers and wooden letter to add missing journaled word on journaled vellum. Mount key cut from transparency on gold textured paper; cover with wooden frame. Paint large letters in green acrylic paint on torn white textured cardstock; ink and mount. Print title on torn vellum; ink edges and mount over painted letters with gold brads.

Jennifer Bourgeault, Macomb Township, Michigan
Photo: Best Side Photo, Grosse Pointe Park, Michigan

Supplies: Patterned vellum, key transparency (Design Originals); green patterned paper (K & Company); gold textured paper (Provo Craft); black and white textured cardstocks (Bazzill); letter stickers (Creative Imaginations); wooden letter, wooden frame (Li'l Davis Designs); letter stencils; brown and black inks; acrylic paint; clear vellum; gold brads; photo corners

Groom

A note written from the groom to the bride adds a personal touch to this groom page. Layer pieces of gold, white mulberry and green patterned paper over ivory patterned paper background. Double mat photos on white metallic paper and textured green cardstock edged with gold leafing; mount. Attach ribbon tied swirl clips on mat. Gold leaf piece of green patterned paper; mount on upper left corner. Embellish with photo charm, letter sticker and word printed on transparency attached with heart brads. Journal on green cardstock; attach with safety pins. Journal on transparency; mount on top of stickers to page with heart brads. Heat emboss metal word and metal frame in gold; adhere word on photos. Print name on green cardstock and mount under embossed frame. Embellish page with photo charm, letter stickers, heart brad and word printed on transparency attached with safety pin.

Natalie Abbott, Lakewood, Colorado
Photos: Lee Bernhard of Colorado Classic Images, Colorado Springs, Colorado

Supplies: White mulberry (Printworks); white metallic swirl paper, gold paper (Paper Adventures); ivory and green patterned papers, textured green cardstock (Crafter's Workshop); mini spiral clips and heart brads (Creative Impressions); photo charm (Nunn Design); gold stickers, stickers (Paper House Productions, Mrs. Grossman's); gold embossing powder; sheer ribbon; transparency; green cardstock; safety pins

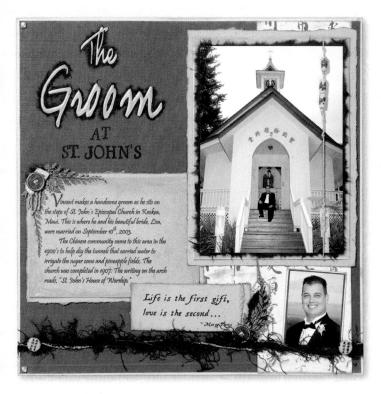

The Groom At St. John's

This page draws inspiration from the church where the wedding took place. Build background by slightly cropping inked textured green cardstock. Attach strips of patterned paper to inked cardstock; mount on tan cardstock background. Journal on beige patterned paper; emboss edges in gold, mat on torn light green speckled cardstock and mount. Print quote on torn light green speckled cardstock; ink edges and wrap with fiber. Embellish corners with leaves, burgundy handmade paper and patterned paper pieces and coins. Triple mat photo on burgundy handmade paper, gold embossed cardstock and light green speckled cardstock. Wrap strung beads around photo; adhere. Double mat smaller photo on textured green and tan cardstocks. String beads on fuzzy fiber; twist with other various fibers and affix across bottom of page. Print "The Groom" title portions on cardstock; emboss, silhouette cut and mat on burgundy handmade paper then mount. Stamp remainder of title.

Michelle Pendleton, Colorado Springs, Colorado
Photos: Rob Ratkowski, Pukalani, Hawaii

Supplies: Green textured cardstock (Bazzill); patterned papers (NRN Designs); burgundy handmade paper (Club Scrap); leaves (Darice); coins (Boxer Scrapbook Productions); letter stamps (Hero Arts); square brads (Making Memories); green, gold and black inks; tan and light green speckled cardstocks; fibers; beads; gold embossing powder

My Groom, My Friend

A love story is spelled out on this clean, balanced layout. Begin by lightly inking blue cardstock background in white. Stitch section of dark blue suede paper on center of page. Print journaling on large torn vellum block; mount over stitched cardstock, placing white cardstock behind journaling and embellishing with pearl beads at corners. Mount photos. Affix title die-cut letters on large vellum metal-rimmed tags; mount. Embellish page with beaded silk flowers.

Cori Dahmen, Portland, Oregon

Supplies: Dark blue suede paper (K & Company); large vellum metal-rimmed tags (Making Memories); die-cut letters (QuicKutz); silk flowers; blue and white cardstocks; white ink; vellum; pearl beads; embroidery floss

And This Woman...

Samantha the Bride

The expression of excitement and wonder on this bride's face is reflected in the warm journaling on the page. Write title and draw rectangle frame on light purple textured cardstock background. Cut circles from light and dark purple textured cardstocks and mount. Mat photo on green textured cardstock; draw frame around mat and mount. Journal on green textured cardstock adding frame; mount. Attach green eyelets on page and on purple cardstock circle mounted with foam tape. Cover "Love" and "mine" metal words in black ink; mount on photo and with silver metal word on page.

Sharon Whitehead, Vernon, British Columbia, Canada

Supplies: Light and dark purple and green textured cardstocks (Bazzill); metal words and eyelets (Making Memories); pen; ruler; black ink; foam tape

Dear Sweetheart

A collaged wedding layout with unique windows reveals pertinent words beneath. Layer word patterned paper, blue mulberry and floral patterned paper on blue cardstock, tearing openings from top two layers to reveal words on paper layers below. Ink torn edges and sew all onto blue cardstock background. Sew frame made from word patterned paper onto photo; embellish with fibers and washers then mat on torn blue mulberry. Sew torn and inked section of cream cardstock to page; mount matted photo atop it. Print journaling on cream cardstock; tear, ink and mount on page with brads. Stamp script images on tags; mat on mulberry. Hang small tags from eyelets set at bottom of photo mat; embellish with metal letters. Mount remaining tag and fiber bow. String metallic thread along edges of page; adorn corners with metal photo corners and lace remnants.

Andrea Lyn Vetten-Marley, Aurora, Colorado

Supplies: Word and floral patterned papers (Me & My Big Ideas, K & Company); blue mulberry paper (DieCuts with a View); washer words, metal photo corners, metal letters (Making Memories); script stamps (PSX Design); blue and cream cardstocks; brown ink; fibers; antique brads; ribbon; metallic thread; lace

In the Bride's Room

A tearful moment stems from a special note written from groom to bride and results in an emotion-packed page. Mat inked and trimmed blue textured cardstock on inked yellow textured cardstock background. Layer sections of patterned and specialty papers and distressed patterned paper on background. Triple mat focal photo on white cardstock, torn mesh paper and corrugated paper; embellish with yellow word ribbon and charm. Wrap vellum envelope with ribbon, insert smaller photo and mount. Print name in large font on green cardstock; print journaling in smaller font over it and mount. Stamp date.

Lindsay Teague, Phoenix, Arizona

Supplies: Yellow, blue and textured cardstocks (Bazzill); patterned papers (KI Memories, Mustard Moon); purple mesh paper (Memory Lane); corrugated paper (Michaels); yellow word ribbon, charm (Making Memories); vellum envelope (EK Success); date stamp; green cardstock; black ink

Mom

A creamy heritage wedding layout showcases yesterday's bride. Mat floral patterned paper on blue cardstock background; mount blue velvet paper page corners and decorative buttons. Mount photo. Tear inner photo frame from blue vellum; chalk edges and mount over photo. Cut second frame from blue cardstock; coat with paper glaze and mini marbles. Adhere atop blue vellum frame. Adhere twisted tulle around frame edge knotting every inch and tying into bow on bottom; add decorative button. Journal on torn vellum; chalk edges and mount. Cut title from blue cardstock; cover in mini marbles and mount over knotted tulle.

Jeanne McKinney, Huntersville, North Carolina

Supplies: Floral patterned paper (Anna Griffin); blue velvet paper (Hobby Lobby); decorative buttons (Jesse James); paper glaze (Duncan); mini marbles (Crafts, Etc.); lettering template (Provo Craft); clear and blue vellums; chalk; blue cardstock; tulle

Grandmother's Portrait

The look of an old painting is achieved by printing this heritage photo onto canvas for a historical wedding page. Begin by painting a thin layer of modeling paste on left and right sides of brown textured cardstock background. When dry, use removable tape to hold a Victorian scroll stencil on modeling paste layer; paint over stencil until covered. Remove stencil and dry. Using foam brush and walnut ink, tint dried paste. Print photo onto canvas photo paper; mat on cream textured cardstock and tie corners with ribbon. Mount. Tint tag with walnut ink; journal. Hang tag from button at top of page.

Kara Wylie, Frisco, Texas

Supplies: Modeling paste (Liquitex); brown and cream textured cardstocks (Bazzill); Victorian swirl stencil (StenSource); walnut ink (7 Gypsies); foam brush; canvas photo paper; ribbon; tag; button

Bride

Use an old wedding photo to inspire a heritage layout. Begin by trimming patterned paper background to 8½ x 11" and set aside. Cut four strips from patterned paper remnant and pleat each strip. Mount pleated strips on back of old photo along edges to form frame; mount framed photo on background paper. Cut tag from distressed cardstock; add pleated paper ribbon. Embellish tag with quilled flower and paper ribbon; mount tag on page.

JoyceAnna DiSclafani, Cherry Hill, New Jersey

Supplies: Patterned paper (Masterpiece Studios); quilling paper (Serendipity Paper); die-cut tag (Accu-Cut); white cardstock

Once Upon a Time

A storytale comes true for this romantic bride on a golden page. Adhere section of gold textured paper at top of floral patterned paper background. Ink edges of white cardstock strip and mount at bottom of gold textured paper; attach twisted tulle and ribbon with brads. Adhere blocks of cardstocks and patterned papers to piece of cardstock to create photo mat. Mount photo on mat with photo corners and mount mat to page. Print title and journaling on white textured cardstock; ink edges. Mat title on burgundy cardstock; attach tulle and ribbon at corners with brads and mount. Embellish journaling box with tulle and ribbon; mount to page.

Colleen Stearns, Natrona Heights, Pennsylvania

Supplies: Gold textured paper (Provo Craft); floral and striped patterned papers (K & Company); green and white textured cardstocks (Bazzill); white and burgundy cardstocks; black ink; ribbon; tulle; brads; brown photo corners

Beautiful Bride

Keep the focus on the bride with a simple but elegant layout. Adhere brown double-sided patterned paper on brown cardstock background folding over opposite corners. Adhere buttons on corners. Double mat photo on plum and white cardstocks leaving room on white mat for title; mount. Apply title with rub-ons. Print poem on white cardstock and mount with eyelets.

Kathryn Allen, Hamilton, Ohio
Photos: Gary & Donna Aufranc, Hamilton, Ohio

Supplies: Brown double-sided patterned paper, word rub-ons (Making Memories); brown and plum cardstocks; buttons; floss; eyelets

Look of Love

Elegant heritage photos need little embellishing on this stunning wedding page. On left side of page, crop bridal photo into sections, mounting each on black cardstock before adhering to brown cardstock background. Mount black cardstock strip vertically on right side of page and top with strips of patterned paper. Set eyelets in patterned paper strips; string fiber. Cover tag with patterned transparency, stamp "the" and embellish with jewels mounted on black cardstock scrap. Hang tag from fiber. Cut title from brown cardstock; mount. Embellish page with jewels, paper roses and pewter heart sticker embossed in gold.

Marpy Hayse, Katy, Texas

Supplies: Patterned paper (Mustard Moon); patterned transparency (ArtChix); letter stamps (Hero Arts); jewels and paper roses (Rubber Baby Buggy Bumpers); pewter heart sticker (Magenta); gold embossing powder; black and brown cardstocks; staples; eyelets

Belle Of The Ball

Quilled embellishments add a delicate touch to this frothy wedding spread. Trim and mount two white textured cardstocks on metallic blue cardstock backgrounds; adhere lace paper atop both pages. On left page, adhere sheer ribbon across top. Cut opening in a piece of cardboard for frame. Wrap frame in blue metallic paper then sheer ribbon. Add flower trim and tulle around frame; mount to page over photo. Fold piece of white cardstock to make title box which can hold a sheet of hidden journaling; mount on page, affixing journaling inside. Embellish with sheer and silk ribbons. Adhere die-cut letters for title; cover with colored dimensional adhesive. Create crystal lacquer flower on wax paper; adorn with jewels. When dry, mount on top of page. On right page, mount strip of lace paper vertically on left side of the page; mount white cardstock piece where the quilled dress will be. Adhere wide sheer ribbon across top and bottom of page and mount double-matted photo. Adorn ribbon with narrower sheer ribbon, folding and adhering as you go to form pleats. Create quilled dress and flowers by following the directions below.

Linda De Los Reyes, Los Gatos, California
Photos: Dennis Way Photography, San Diego, California

Supplies: White textured cardstock (Making Memories); metallic blue cardstock (Canson); lace paper (Artistic Scrapper); die-cut letters (QuicKutz); dimensional glue (Ranger); crystal lacquer (Sakura Hobby Craft); jewels (Darice); quilling tool (Serendipity Paper); sheer ribbon; cardboard; flower trim; tulle; silk ribbon; quilling strips.

1 Create the quilled wedding dress embellishment with a quilling tool and quilling paper strips. Roll quilling strips into tiny tight circular shapes. Adhere together to form bodice shape.

2 Create skirt portion of quilled dress design by forming loops from quilling strips. Adhere into place on cardstock below quilled bodice section.

Beautiful

This wedding layout reflects the beauty of a young bride in its simple elegance. Wrap tulle around bottom of black textured paper; gather in front off-center and attach on page with silver concho. Mount photo. Tear metallic paper; mount, covering corner of photo. Apply rub-on word title.

Lindsay Teague, Phoenix, Arizona

Supplies: Black textured paper (Memory Lane); silver concho (Scrapworks); metallic paper (Hot Off The Press); rub-on word (Making Memories); tulle

This Day I Thee Wed

As elegant as a bride on her wedding day, this page shimmers. Paint decorative tin with white acrylic paint; cut out center to create frame. Mount on black cardstock background. Adhere black trim around frame window. Print photo on canvas photo paper and mount. Adorn tin with sequins and pearl beads. Apply title using rub-ons affixed onto transparency; crop and mount on tin sheet.

Kara Wylie, Frisco, Texas
Photo: AspenLight Photography, Dallas, Texas

Supplies: Decorative tin (Artistic Expressions); rub-on letters and word ribbon (Making Memories); white acrylic paint; black cardstock; black trim; canvas photo paper; sequins; pearl beads; transparency

Butterfly Kisses

A patchwork layout of inked patterned papers frames this stunning bride. Ink edges of cut patterned papers and mount on two pieces of black cardstock background. Mat photos on white cardstock; ink edges. Mount focal photo on left page with red satin page corners. Print title and journaling on white cardstock; crop and ink edges. Double mat on patterned paper and black cardstock. Align background pages and mount title block and one matted photo so they stride the pages; carefully cut along seam. Mount remaining matted photo on right page. Embellish with butterfly charms.

Denise Tucker, Versailles, Indiana
Photos: Brooke Tarvin Photography, Shreveport, Louisiana

Supplies: Patterned papers (Anna Griffin, Frances Meyer, K & Company, 7 Gypsies); red satin page corners (Anna Griffin); butterfly charms (Eggery Place); black and white cardstocks; black ink

Joy

The feelings of this bride are reflected in her glowing face and the page title. Tear red floral and green leaf patterned paper; mount on striped patterned paper background. Mount torn pieces of white floral patterned paper. Double mat photo on white and red cardstocks; tear bottom of red mat and mount. Add title and embellish with heart plaque.

Sharon Bissett O' Neal, Lee's Summit, Missouri

Supplies: Red and white floral and striped patterned papers (Colorbök); green leaf patterned paper (EK Success); heart plaque (Making Memories); white and red cardstocks

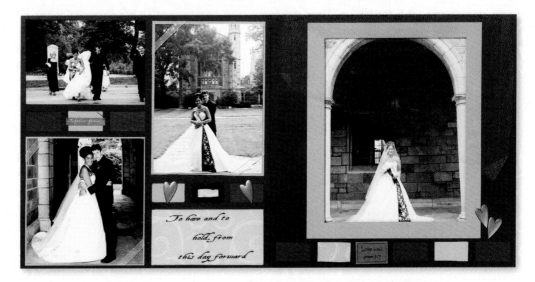

To Have and To Hold

A section of bridal veil embellishes this bold wedding layout. Use color blocking template to determine placement of photos and embellishments. Cut openings in black cardstock to create overlay. On left page, mat two photos on gray cardstock and wrap corners with sheer ribbon. Mount both on top of black cardstock overlay. Adhere sections of red cardstock and title printed on vellum on gray cardstock background; cover with overlay and embellish with heart and word charms and beads. On right page, cut openings in black cardstock for overlay. Frame large opening with gray cardstock; sew on piece from veil. Use foam adhesive to mount enlarged photo on underside of framed opening. Adhere sections of gray and red cardstocks and patterned vellum on back of black cardstock overlay openings. Embellish with plaque and heart charms.

Anna Burgess, Clarksville, Tennessee
Photos: Gem Photography, Jackson, Michigan

Supplies: Color blocking template (Deluxe Designs); patterned vellum (source unknown); heart charms, plaque (Making Memories); word charm (Scrap-Ease); beads (Magic Scraps); black, red and gray cardstocks; sheer white ribbon

Andrea's Wedding

An enlarged photo surrounded by smaller supporting photos creates a dramatic wedding spread. Enlarge photo. Apply title and journaling directly onto photo and mount across two cardstock backgrounds; cut center seam. Print smaller photos and rose clip art; mount. Decoratively cut borders and frame from red cardstock and mount. Embellish page with rose clip art.

Dana Forti, Claremont, California

Supplies: Decorative scissors (Fiskars); black and red cardstocks; rose clip art

The Bride

A moment of quiet and reflection is the calming focus of this peaceful page. Tear border from floral patterned paper and mount vertically on cream cardstock background. Triple mat photo on green cardstock and floral patterned paper; adhere to page. Affix floral sticker on tag; set eyelet and tie with fibers and ribbon before mounting on page with foam adhesive. Print title and journaling on brown cardstock; crop to tag shape, set eyelet and embellish with ribbon and sticker. Mount.

Reeca Davis Marotz, Idaho Falls, Idaho

Supplies: Floral patterned paper (Anna Griffin); floral stickers (Gifted Line); ribbon (Offray); small tag die cut (Accu-Cut); cream, green and brown cardstocks; eyelets; fibers; foam adhesive; sheer plaid ribbon

Blushing Bride

Flower petals made from torn pieces of card-stock seem to flutter from the bride's bouquet on this pretty page. Print title on bottom of purple cardstock background. Affix purple patterned paper piece vertically on left side of page. Tear pieces of cream cardstock into petal shapes and mount. Mat photo on white card-stock and adhere over petals.

Heather Melzer, Yorkville, Illinois
Photo: Shelby Valadez, Saugus, California

Supplies: Purple patterned paper (Mustard Moon); purple, cream and white cardstocks

"Suddenly, quietly, you realize that - from this moment
forth - you will no longer walk through this life alone.
like a new sun this awareness arises within you, freeing
you from fear, opening your life. It is the beginning of love,
and the end of all that came before."

Robert Frost

March 6, 2004

Sylvia

A quote from Robert Frost and a single photo showcase the bride on this wedding day page. Turn 8½ x 11" ivory textured cardstock background 90 degrees; print quote on bottom left corner and date on bottom right corner. Cut section from patterned paper; mount on top of page. Mount ribbon across lower edge of patterned paper; adorn with large brads. Add handcut title. Create mat by following the directions below. Mount on page.

Becky Thompson, Fruitland, Idaho

Supplies: Patterned paper (Anna Griffin); ivory and red textured cardstocks (Bazzill); ribbon (Offray); gold embossing powder; large brads

1 To create the unique photo mat, cut a piece of paper slightly wider than your photo. Use removable adhesive to mount a piece of paper in the middle of the mat to "hold" the spot in which your photo will later be mounted. Tear the mat's edges to create a frayed edge. Gently roll the torn edges upward to create a border. Work around the mat until all sides are rolled.

2 Remove the paper "holding piece" from the mat and, using a watermark pad, lightly ink the torn edges. Sprinkle with embossing powder and heat to set. Mount photo inside curled edges.

20 Years' Experience

A layout showcasing "then and now" photos speaks to ripening love. Begin by matting two pieces of burgundy embossed paper on black textured cardstock backgrounds. Enhance torn pieces of patterned vellum with metallic rub-ons and mount in corners. Double mat photos on black cardstock and gold textured paper; mount with foam adhesive. Strap sheer ribbons across photos; affix on pages with decorative corners. Print dates on beige cardstock; mount on photos under label holders. Create envelope from patterned vellum; enhance with metallic rub-ons and adhere on right page with foam adhesive. Journal on beige cardstock. Enhance edges with metallic rub-ons; mount label holder. Slip journaling in envelope. Print title on transparency; gold emboss and heat set. String rings from title with fiber; mount.

Denise Tucker, Versailles, Indiana
Photos: Robert Huddle Photography, Galesburg, Illinois

Supplies: Burgundy embossed paper, gold textured paper (Provo Craft); patterned vellum (Daisy D's); metallic rub-ons (Craf-T); decorative corners (Eggery Place); label holder (Boutique Trims); rings (Wilton); gold embossing powder; black cardstock; foam adhesive; sheer ribbon; transparency; fibers

With This Hand

A variety of stamped images adds a delicate touch to this hand-in-hand layout. Use watermark ink to stamp iris flowers onto sienna cardstock background and pieces of pink and tan cardstocks. Chalk edges of torn pink and tan stamped pieces and layer on background. Adhere mesh strip. Mat photo on tan cardstock; mount. Stamp title letters on cardstock squares; emboss and heat set before mounting. Stamp tag images; chalk. Adhere torn vellum on top of fiber-tied tag; journal and mount. Stamp small phrase on tan cardstock, write date and adhere below photo.

Nicole La Cour, Memory Makers magazine

Supplies: Iris flower stamps, background stamp, title letter stamps, small letter stamps (Prickley Pear); watermark ink (Tsukineko); mesh (Magic Scraps); clear embossing powder; sienna, tan, pink and white cardstocks; chalk; vellum

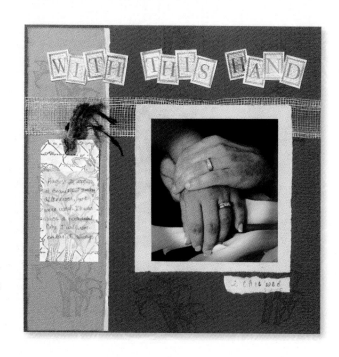

The Rings

The bridal bouquet dictated the colors for this blooming layout. Begin by mounting sections of patterned paper on pink textured cardstock background. Mat photo on mauve textured cardstock; mount. Create title with heart-shaped bubble letter stickers. Wrap fibers around bottom of page. Stamp date.

Amanda Huntington, Seminole, Florida

Supplies: Patterned paper (Paper Adventures); pink and mauve textured cardstocks (Bazzill); heart-shaped bubble letter stickers (Creative Imaginations); date stamp (Making Memories); fibers; silver ink

Promises

A preprinted transparency makes a poignant photo overlay on this powerful page. Mount pieces of tan patterned paper on red patterned paper background. Attach transparency on photo with small brads; mount. Attach silk flower with large decorative brad. Cover decorative metal-rimmed tag with red patterned paper; tie ribbon and mount. Apply title on tag with die-cut letters.

Diana Hudson, Bakersfield, California
Photo: Kelli Noto, Centennial, Colorado

Supplies: Red and tan patterned papers, decorative metal-rimmed tag (Creative Imaginations); preprinted transparency (Carolee's Creations); large decorative brad (Making Memories); die-cut letters (QuicKutz); silk flower; small brads; ribbon

Hand in Hand Forever

This wedding page seems to bloom with flower embellishments. Print "Forever" portion of title and journaling on pink textured cardstock. Cut hole in pink textured cardstock to make frame; tear edges and roll. Mount photo on periwinkle cardstock background; print names on torn pink vellum and adhere across photo. Mount pink cardstock frame section atop photo and background page. Tear strip of pink vellum; mount on left side of page. Tear corner section from pink embossed paper; roll edges and adhere at bottom of page. Cut heart from cardstock and insert in pink vellum envelope; embellish with ribbon, flower sticker and heart charm before mounting. Affix purple letter stickers on pink embossed paper section for "Heart"; add flower stickers. Print "Hand" and "To" on vellum; adhere to portions of floral photos. Mount to page under metal-rimmed beribboned tags. String sheer ribbon through eyelets set in three page corners and tie at top with printed date tag. Embellish page with silk flowers.

Kathy Fesmire, Athens, Tennessee
Photo: Portraits By Cheri Ellis, Cleveland, Tennessee

Supplies: Pink textured cardstock, pink embossed paper (Paper Adventures); pink vellum envelope (EK Success); purple letter and flower stickers (K & Company); heart charm (Card Connection); black letter stickers (Wordsworth); silk flowers; periwinkle cardstock; pink vellum; sheer ribbon; metal-rimmed tags; eyelets

Our Second Chance

Love is special the second time around, as witnessed in this subtle but beautiful page. Layer mauve and purple patterned papers on ivory patterned paper background. Mat photo on purple patterned paper; adhere torn patterned paper scrap at photo's bottom. Embellish with silk bow; mount. Journal on silver vellum; mount. Adhere frame cut-out on page around smaller photo. Affix tiny photo charm; mount. Apply title with epoxy letter stickers, die-cut letters and stamped and embossed letters matted on silver patterned paper.

Holle Wiktorek, Reunion, Colorado

Supplies: Mauve, purple and ivory patterned papers, frame cut-out (Anna Griffin); frame, epoxy letter stickers (Li'l Davis Designs); die-cut letters (QuicKutz); letter stamps (La Pluma); silver embossing powder; ribbon; silver vellum

With This Ring, I Thee Wed

Cut identical window openings from a sheet of tagboard and a piece of foam core. Set aside foam core. For left page, cover both front and back of tagboard with white textured paper. Cut vellum to mount on top of white textured paper, trimming away small border around window opening to expose underlying white textured paper; treat exposed white paper with silver leafing pen. Create the frame following the directions below. Print title on transparency; sprinkle with silver embossing powder, heat to set, and adhere. For right page, mount vellum to foam core previously covered in white textured paper. To create background, mount vellum sheet on top of white textured cardstock and mount behind foam core window. Embellish with glove and journaling. Attach foam core to front page using joint tape as hinge.

Jenny Moore Lowe, Lafayette, Colorado
Photos: Owens Photography

Supplies: White textured cardstock (Bazzill); patterned papers (NRN Designs); silver embossing powder (Hero Arts); silver leafing pen (Krylon); beads; tape; metallic thread; foam core board; joint tape

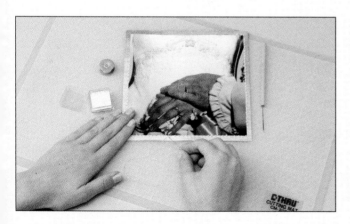

1 Mat photo on white textured cardstock colored with silver leafing pen. Pierce holes around edge of photo mat. Pass threaded needle through a hole, through a bead, then back through the same hole. Repeat around entire photo.

2 Punch holes and add beads around entire border. Using tape, attach both the border and center photo to a square grid, lining up all four sides, placing the photo in the center of the border. Using a figure 8 pattern, wrap metallic thread around the beads, moving from the outside of the frame toward the inside. Embellish back of photo mat with additional matted photo.

In the Presence of Family and Friends...

Memories

A handmade mini photo album allows for display of additional flower girl photos on this unique page. Tear corner and bottom from floral patterned paper; mount on cream cardstock background. Mount photos on bottom of page; embellish with decorative buttons. Adhere title letter brads above photos. Mount focal photo on peach cardstock; ink edges. Wrap lace ribbon with charm around photo; mount. Cut cream cardstock to book size. Embellish cover with inked squares of floral and harlequin paper. Affix inked definition sticker on cover; adhere bow. Create pages for book from torn floral patterned and harlequin paper mounted on cream cardstock; mount book to background page with hinges and brads. Mount photo in book.

Mary Bautista Marty, Chula Vista, California

Supplies: Floral patterned paper (Anna Griffin); letter brads (Colorbök); ribbon charm, hinges, definition sticker (Making Memories); harlequin paper (Daisy Hill); cream cardstock; decorative buttons; black ink; brads

Bride Bliss

A shining moment between a bride and her bridesmaids shines within a metallic frame. Sew two torn sections of patterned paper on gray textured cardstock background. Attach lace bow adorned with silk flower. Apply title directly on photo with rub-on words. Embellish tin frame with white acrylic paint; tuck photo inside. Mount framed photo over lace, wrapping left side of lace across frame. Journal on transparency; sew onto tag. Mount on page and adorn with silk flower and brad.

Patricia Anderson, Selah, Washington
Photos: Yuen Lui, Seattle, Washington

Supplies: Gray textured cardstock, patterned paper, tag (Chatterbox); silk flowers (Hirschberg Schutz & Co.); rub-on words (Making Memories); tin frame (Artistic Expressions); lace; brads; transparency; white acrylic paint

Beautiful Flower Girls

Flower girls look perfectly pretty in their matching dresses on this perfectly pretty page. Tear bottom edge from patterned paper; sew onto pink textured cardstock background. Print partial title on transparency and mount under torn photo edge. Frame photo with lace; embellish corners with silk flowers and brads. Apply names on tags with letter stickers; tie ribbon and adhere on corners. Journal on transparency; mount on bottom of page. Apply remaining title with rub-on word.

Patricia Anderson, Selah, Washington
Photos: Yuen Lui, Seattle, Washington

Supplies: Patterned paper, pink textured cardstocks, tags, letter stickers (Chatterbox); word rub-ons (Making Memories); silk flowers (Hirschberg, Schutz, & Co.); ribbon; transparency

Brooke and Mariah were absolutely adorable as our little flower girls. Brooke was six, and Mariah was five at the time. They loved getting all dressed up in their mini brides' dresses complete with white gloves and pink

Flower Girl

Cottony texture and petal pink set the mood for this wanna-touch wedding layout. Tear edges of handmade white floral paper; lightly chalk flowers and mat on pink textured cardstock. Mount photo. Tear frame opening from piece of pink handmade paper; roll edges, tie with ribbon and mount over photo. Embellish frame with fiber and metal decorative frame displaying date stamped on handmade paper scrap. Journal on transparency and mount below photo. Cover title letter stickers in watercolor crayon and mount with pressed flower; cover with mica tile. Affix metal decorative photo corners on smaller photo. Mat on mica tile and handmade paper scrap; mount. Adhere pressed flower on page. Wrap loose silk flower petals and pearls in tulle; twist and tie with fiber and ribbon. Mount with flower push pins; attach pin in upper left page corner.

Jeniece Higgins, Lake Forest, Illinois

Supplies: Pink textured cardstock; (Bazzill); handmade flower paper (source unknown); pink handmade paper (source unknown); letter stamps (Hero Arts); metal decorative frame, photo corners (Nunn Design); letter stickers (Creative Imaginations); watercolor crayons (Waterman); mica tiles (USArtQuest); flower push pins (Target); chalk; ribbon; fuzzy fiber; transparency; loose silk flower petals; pressed flowers; tulle; pearls

Flower Girl

A beautiful digital layout is created in Photoshop by framing a photo of the flower girl and bride. Begin by creating a frame and background for your page using the Saint Patrick's Day and pearl kits from the Web site noted below. Use the hue/saturation and color balance filters to create desired effect. Drag and drop the frame onto the background paper. Add photograph on a layer below the frame layer; merge layers. To create first part of title, download the Foil Alphabet from Web site noted below and select letters using the rectangular marquee tool; drag onto page. Open Pearl Strands file from the pearl kit; drag and drop pearls onto layout resizing as necessary. Add the fiber and claddaugh charm from the Saint Patrick's Day kit on a layer below the pearls. To create the vellum journal box, on a separate layer create a vertical rectangle with the rectangular marquee tool; fill with white and lower the opacity of the layer to 20 percent. Add a shadow and slight texture in the layer style dialog box. Using horizontal type tool, draw a box to type in and journal. Add the second part of title by using a larger font; colorize with the eyedropper tool using the background color. Adjust the bevel and emboss in the layer style dialog box. Apply additional shadowing on each layer to achieve realistic look.

Doris Castle, Fonda, New York
Photo: Carol Bluestein Photography, Slingerlands, New York

Supplies: Photoshop (Adobe); Saint Patrick's Day and pearl kits, foil alphabet (www.pagesoftheheart.com)

Nana's Charms

Digital paper provides a lush background for this layout created in Photoshop. Download the background paper from Web site noted below. Download the images of charms and pin; rotate each of the charms differently to make them appear to hang. Add photo and apply an opaque shadow to draw the eye downward across the layout. Journal.

Doris Castle, Fonda, New York
Photo: Carol Bluestein Photography, Slingerlands, New York

Supplies: Photoshop (Adobe); background paper, pins and charms (www.pagesoftheheart.com)

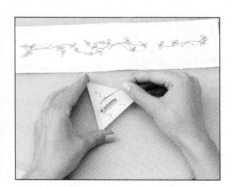

Only You

Trudy uses stitching and beadwork to create a border that complements the beauty of the little girl in the layout. Trim peach cardstock to mat on darker textured cardstock background; crumple, flatten out, and mount on background page. Double mat photo; adhere on page adorning corners with silver photo corners. Print journaling on light peach cardstock; cut into two tags and a journaling box. Mat journaling on textured cardstock and adhere under photo. Frame tags with a hand-drawn line, set eyelet in top, tie off with ribbon, and slip inside organza bag. Adhere trim around bottom of bag and mount on page at bottom corner of photo. Embellish bag with key and fabric label. Create floral beaded border by following the directions below.

Trudy Sigurdson, Victoria, British Columbia, Canada
Photo: Kelli Noto, Centennial, Colorado

Supplies: Mulberry paper (Pulsar); silver photo corners (Canson); organza bag (source unknown); key (Quest Beads); fabric label (Me & My Big Ideas); peach and textured peach cardstocks; lace trim; floss; beads; black pen; eyelets

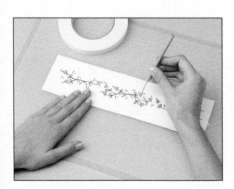

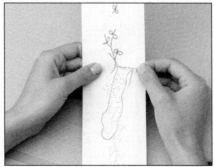

1 To create floral beaded border draw a pattern on a paper strip. Temporarily adhere to mulberry strip mounted on pink cardstock strip. Pierce holes through pattern and cardstock to create sewing guide. Remove the pattern.

2 Hand stitch stems and leaves with green embroidery floss using a backstitch.

3 Sew pink and white seed beads to the stitched design to embellish. Add lace trim to the right side and mount on page.

Love of My Life

This timeless layout showcases a relationship destined to last. Create background by layering patterned papers and pink, gray and tan cardstock sections onto green cardstock background. Mat photo on green cardstock, adhering torn and chalked strip at top with gingham ribbon and charm; mount with decorative photo corner. Wrap word ribbon at bottom of page; apply rub-on words. Chalk definition stickers and mount. Stamp date and title on distressed cardstock; mount bookplate over date and title over pink cardstock block. Attach ribbon tied spiral holder at upper corner of page with brads. Embellish spiral with chalked word blocks; embellish page with decorative corner and page turn.

Nicole Quinn, Eagle River, Alaska

Supplies: Patterned papers (Anna Griffin, My Mind's Eye, 7 Gypsies); ribbon charm, word ribbon, rub-on words, definition stickers, date stamp (Making Memories); decorative photo corners (source unknown); photo turn, spiral holder (7 Gypsies); letter stamps (Hero Arts, PSX Design, Wordsworth); pink, gray and tan cardstocks; chalk; gingham ribbon; label holder

Shelby and Lanie

A special wedding day is graced by a special relationship between the bride and flower girl, as seen on this stunning spread. Ink a cream textured cardstock background. Adhere patterned vellum strip to page left. Ink pieces of flower patterned paper, script patterned paper, frame and embroidered paper photo mat. Mount photo atop mat and wrap with ribbon; layer onto page with inked papers, strips, ribbon and frame. Stamp descriptive words onto flower patterned paper and names on ribbon and frame.

Shelby Valadez, Saugus, California

Supplies: Cream textured cardstock, flower patterned vellum and paper frame (Chatterbox); script patterned paper (7 Gypsies); embroidered paper (Jennifer Collection); stamps (PSX Design, Stampers Anonymous); brown ink; ribbon

Special Moments

A mother/daughter moment is the focus of this captivating wedding page. Begin with striped patterned paper background. Mat photo on purple textured cardstock with metal photo corner and word accent; mount. Print title on vellum; emboss. Cut title into two pieces and mount around photo. Journal on torn cream cardstock; mount. Embellish journaling box with skeleton leaves and decorative button.

Sonya Pritchard, Atherton, Queensland, Australia

Supplies: Striped patterned paper (Chatterbox); purple textured cardstock (Bazzill); metal photo corner (Arbee Crafts); metal word accent (DieCuts with a View); skeleton leaves; embossing powder; brads; vellum; cream cardstock; decorative button

Sweet Girl

A special mother/daughter photo is the foundation for this special layout. Ink edges of cream cardstock strip; adhere vertically on page. Mount velvet ribbon on strip; add printed date mounted under decorative frame. Mat photo on inked pink textured cardstock; layer on background with small inked pink rectangle and black textured cardstock. Journal on cream cardstock; ink edges and mount. Affix definition with brads atop oval tag, torn and inked pink textured cardstock and inked patterned tag. Tie with ribbon and mount.

Becky Novacek, Fremont, Nebraska
Photo: Tom Novacek, Fremont, Nebraska

Supplies: Decorative frame (www.twopeasinabucket.com); green, pink and black textured cardstocks (Bazzill); definition, oval tag, patterned tag (Foofala); cream cardstock; black ink; velvet ribbon

Tired Tootsies

The lighter side of a wedding is featured on this easygoing page. Print journaling and partial title on purple textured cardstock; mount on top half of green textured cardstock background. Finish title with letter stickers; adhere page pebble over "o." Mount strip of patterned paper across center of page and section of yellow textured cardstock to bottom half of background. Mat photo on light purple textured cardstock; mount. Embellish with page pebbles adhered to patterned paper.

Kimberly Lund, Wichita, Kansas
Photo: Dan Lund, Wichita, Kansas

Supplies: Purple, green, light purple and yellow textured cardstocks (Bazzill); patterned paper, letter stickers (Chatterbox); page pebbles (Making Memories)

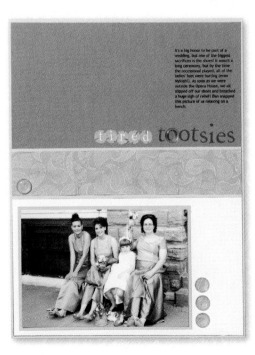

The Bearer of All Rings

A ring bearer's job is both exciting and a little intimidating, as seen on this lively spread. Layer sections of patterned papers and blue cardstock on two blue cardstock backgrounds. For left page, triple mat focal photo on blue cardstock and patterned paper; apply decorative metal corners and mount. Print name and date on torn vellum and mount with brads. Apply letter sticker title. Embellish page with sheer ribbon bow mounted over mesh. On right page, mat photos on blue and tan cardstocks; mount. Journal on torn vellum; mount on page with brads. Insert stamped word in metal-rimmed tag. Affix micro beads around metal rim adding heart charms; layer on page with tied sheer ribbon and mesh.

Barb Hogan, Cincinnati, Ohio
Photo: Catherine Noland, Aurora, Illinois

Supplies: Patterned papers (Creative Imaginations); cardstocks; vellum; brads; sheer ribbon; micro beads; black ink

One Last Kiss for Luck

A funny photo is the focus of this beautifully embellished page. Layer torn black textured cardstock and patterned papers on patterned background page; wrap ribbon around top and tie in a bow. Double mat photo on patterned paper and black textured cardstock. Tie sheer ribbons through eyelets along edge of mat; mount. Journal on white cardstock; mat on torn black textured cardstock and mount. Cover torn black cardstock hearts with mesh and mount with gold paper scraps and decorative buttons. Create title with die-cut letters and letter cut-outs.

Holle Wiktorek, Reunion, Colorado
Photo: Narcissus Magturo of NAM Photography, Ft. Leonard Wood, Missouri

Supplies: Black textured cardstock (DMD); patterned papers (Anna Griffin); stitched ribbon (Magic Scraps); mesh (Magenta); gold paper (Crafts, Etc.); die-cut letters (QuicKutz); letter cut-outs (Daisy D's); decorative buttons (Blumenthal Lansing); eyelets; sheer ribbons

My Mother, My Friend

A photo of the bride and her mother are showcased in an elegant pearled frame. Begin by double matting photo on cream metallic handmade paper and black cardstock; mount on shiny cream cardstock background. Line outside edges of frame with double-sided tape and adhere pearl beads. Print title on metallic handmade paper; cut into two rectangular tags. Mat tags on black cardstock. Set eyelets and tie together with paper yarn; mount.

Kara Wylie, Frisco, Texas
Photo: Ernie Owens, Arlington, Texas

Supplies: Paper yarn (Making Memories); cream metallic handmade paper (Emagination Crafts); pearl beads (Westrim); shiny cream cardstock (source unknown); double-sided tape; black cardstock; eyelets

Today...

A simple layout provides emotional impact for these beautiful black-and-white photos. Create title and journaling on white cardstock background using varied fonts. Mat and mount black-and-white photos and mount to right side of background. Embellish with punched flowers and stems tied with silver thread.

Cheryl Bahneman, Acworth, Georgia
Photos: Matt Hall of Hall Studio, Marietta, Georgia

Supplies: Flower punch (Marvy); white cardstock; silver thread

Who Gives This Woman

Tags supply a perfect platform for journaled thoughts of the bride and her father on this lovely page. Layer light blue textured cardstock and denim weave patterned paper on denim textured cardstock background. Stitch around edge of page and along edge of denim weave patterned paper. Mount photo. Tear flower patterned paper for bottom page border; mount and fold back top torn edge. Adhere a torn section of denim weave paper on flowered border. Stitch around page and border section again. Apply title letter stickers. Adhere fiber and definition twill tape at top of page. Journal on paper tags; hang from metal-rimmed tags, embellishing with heart charm and silk and metal flower. Affix "I remember" on page with letter stickers.

Kari Barrera, Warrenton, Virginia

Supplies: Light blue and denim textured cardstocks, denim weave patterned paper, flower patterned paper (Chatterbox); letter stickers (Chatterbox, Creative Imaginations, Wordsworth); definition twill tape (7 Gypsies); silk and metal flower (Making Memories); heart charm (source unknown); fiber; metal-rimmed tags

The Girls

A relaxed photo of the girls in the wedding party is featured on this easygoing page. Mount green cardstock strip at bottom of floral patterned paper background. Mount patterned paper strips on top of page and top edge of green cardstock strip. Double mat photo on white and lavender cardstocks; mount. Print title onto heart-shaped vellum tag. Hang tag from eyelet set in patterned paper strip; secure to page with heart-shaped swirl clip.

Sharon Bissett O' Neal, Lee's Summit, Missouri

Supplies: Floral and striped patterned papers (Colorbök); heart-shaped vellum tag, heart-shaped clip (Making Memories); green, lavender and white cardstocks; eyelet

The Guys

Men will be boys even on a wedding day, as featured in this no-sweat layout. Mat photo on sage cardstock; tear bottom edge. Mount over green patterned paper block onto striped patterned paper background. Print title on vellum tag. Hang tag from eyelet set on cardstock mat.

Sharon Bissett O' Neal, Lee's Summit, Missouri

Supplies: Green and striped patterned papers (Anna Griffin); vellum tag (Making Memories); sage cardstock; eyelet

Ring Bearer

This adorable photo is showcased in a layout that draws focus to the child's concentration. Tear section of blue marbled patterned paper; mount on striped patterned paper background. Mat cut section of swirl patterned paper on white cardstock; adhere on bottom of page. Print name and title on torn vellum; mount name on photo. Attach title onto border with brads.

Sharon Bissett O'Neal, Lee's Summit, Missouri

Supplies: Striped patterned paper (Colorbök); blue marble paper (source unknown); swirl patterned paper (Frances Meyer); vellum; brads

Best Friends

A black-and-white photo is complemented with lively lavender papers on this simple but effective page. Mount sections of leaf and striped patterned papers on floral patterned paper. Double mat photo on white and lavender cardstocks. Cut slits in mat edges and wrap strings around mat and through slits. Write date on vellum tag and tie onto mat; mount matted photo. Print title on torn vellum and mount.

Sharon Bissett O' Neal, Lee's Summit, Missouri

Supplies: Leaf, striped and floral patterned papers (Colorbōk); vellum tag (Making Memories); lavender and white cardstocks; string; vellum

Just Married

The best parts of a busy photo are embraced with digitally created overlay frames in this goin' places page. Begin by creating a new document in Photoshop CS. Fill first layer with white; add sandstone texture. Add second layer drawing a rectangle with the marquee tool; fill with a desired color. Add noise with the noise filter and a drop shadow using layer effects. Create third layer filling the area with a cream color; repeat the noise and drop shadow. Create torn edge of mat by erasing portions and then painting back in the white edge. Repeat on a fourth layer with black, and on fifth layer to make the photo mat using a sandstone texture filter. Paste photo using a sixth layer; add drop shadow. Create new layer; using the marquee tool, draw a rectangle to act as a frame for the photo. Add a thick stroke of the cream color to create frame and add the same filter treatments and drop shadow as the paper layers. Add a new layer and repeat previous steps to create the horizontal frame. Erase the small section of the horizontal frame where it overlaps the vertical one so it appears that they are intertwined. Add journaling captions in the open areas in the frames. Create title using individual letter brushes. Apply slight de-bossing so the letters appear stamped onto the textured paper. Using marquee tool, draw a small square, fill, and apply a metallic filter. Duplicate square brad as necessary and arrange as indicated. Apply additional shadowing on each layer as necessary to achieve realistic look.

Tonya Doughty, Wenatchee, Washington

Supplies: Photoshop CS (Adobe)

A Quiet Moment

The focal photo featured on this layout is reinforced with angular paper elements and a well-chosen color combination. Cut long triangles and strips of fuchsia, dark pink and purple cardstocks; mount on light pink cardstock background. Triple mat photo and mount. Punch flowers from yellow, white and pink cardstocks; adhere on page. Print title and journaling on vellum and mount before embellishing with punched flowers.

Mary Faith Roell, Harrison, Ohio

Supplies: Flower punch (EK Success); fuchsia, dark pink, light pink, purple, yellow and white cardstocks; vellum

The Best and Most Beautiful Things

A quote from Helen Keller conveys this bride's feelings about a special child who shared her wedding day celebrations. Mat photos on triangle pieces cut from deep red cardstock; mount on patterned paper background. Print text on cream cardstock; cut into sections and mat on tan and deep red cardstocks. Embellish with punched hearts, eyelets and fibers, pearl bead strand, angel and bee charms and decorative brads.

Linda Cummings, Murfreesboro, Tennessee
Photos: Tracy Ray Shuey, Murfreesboro, Tennessee

Supplies: Patterned paper (Provo Craft); angel charm (source unknown); bee charm (Boutique Trims); decorative brads (www.memoriesoftherabbit.com); heart punch; deep red, cream and tan cardstocks; eyelets; fibers; pearl bead strand

Bridesmaid, My Friend...

The emotions of a bride's sister are as poignant as this computer-generated page is powerful. Create the layout using a large background photo. Create the vellum effect by creating a pattern on a separate image layer, then lowering the opacity. Crop and re-size photos on bottom; align with no matting over the bottom pattern. Create the title on a separate layer; reduce opacity to better blend with the background. Add two patterned paper strips and a vellum journaling block with text.

Sally Beacham, East Waterboro, Maine

Supplies: Paint Shop Pro 8.1 (Jasc)

Where There is Love

This digital layout incorporates a diverse range of wedding photos on a fanciful page. First, create a custom template for the color-blocked layout using the picture frame tool. Add all the photos under the template and re-size and position them as needed. Create a variety of textures to make the frame template and other sections of the layout look like textured cardstock. Give the top corner photo a "pastel sketch" effect and add embellishments created from one of your own flower photos. To make the names and title tags, create cut-out text on the tag and title block using built-in effects in Paint Shop Pro 8.

Sally Beacham, East Waterboro, Maine

Supplies: Paint Shop Pro 8.1 (Jasc)

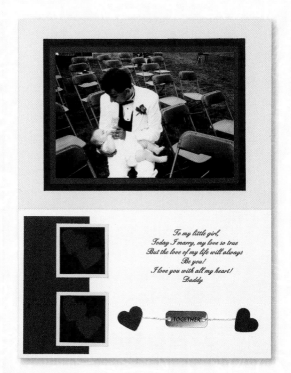

To My Little Girl

A sweet poem and heartwarming photo convey a groom's tender feelings for his baby girl on this loving page. Print poem on bottom half of white cardstock background; mount section from gray cardstock on top half of background. Double mat photo on burgundy and black cardstocks; mount on gray cardstock background. Punch hearts from burgundy cardstock; double mat on black and white cardstock squares and mount on rectangle burgundy cardstock block. Mount metal tag with fiber and punched hearts on page.

Jamy Podluzne, Geneva, Ohio

Supplies: Heart punch (Carl); metal tag (source unknown); white, gray, burgundy and black cardstocks; fiber

Do You Take This Person...

The Aisle

A memorable moment for this bride and her father was captured forever on this powerful page. Cut strips and circles from patterned paper, gold textured paper and burgundy cardstock. Mount select cut pieces on cream textured cardstock background. Mat focal photo on cream cardstock and smaller photo on gold textured paper. Layer matted photos on mounted cut pieces, leaving the center portion of the larger photo free so journaling tag can later be slipped behind. Mount un-matted photo. Embellish page with swirl clips, square brads and satin bow. Create title with gold leafed wooden letters and letter stickers. Journal on ivory cardstock; mat on burgundy cardstock and tie metallic thread through punched hole. Slip behind photo.

Jennifer Bourgeault, Macomb Township, Michigan
Photos: Best Side Photo, Grosse Pointe Park, Michigan

Supplies: Patterned paper (Chatterbox); gold textured paper, textured background paper (Provo Craft); wooden letters (Li'l Davis Designs); letter stickers (All My Memories); gold leafing pen (Krylon); silk bow (Anna Griffin); burgundy and ivory cardstocks; swirl clips; square brads; metallic thread

The Processional

A simple and elegant wedding layout is created in Photoshop. Begin by opening a new document; open up photos and place in document using the move tool. Using eyedropper tool, select color from the photos to use as background; create a new layer and fill background layer with paint bucket tool. Create a new layer; choose another color to use as the second background. Using marquee tool, draw out a square that is slightly smaller than your original background. Fill your background layer with the second color. Use the layer styles to add slight shadow to the second background layer. Open up a floral photo; using move tool, drag it onto your page and place it near page bottom. Hit CTRL/U to colorize using the sliders to achieve desired effect. Add text onto your document. Add shadows. On your main photo, using the marquee tool, hold down the shift key as you drag to keep it square selecting the area of the photo you would like to keep. Click on Select/Inverse and hit delete to get rid of the unwanted photo area. Using layer styles, do a stroke to mat and add a shadow to your main photo.

Amanda Behrmann, Austin, Texas

Supplies: Photoshop (Adobe)

Because You Loved Me

This musical layout rings with romance. Print sheet music onto white cardstock; tear edges and mount on printed background paper. Smear modeling paste around edges and ink with walnut ink. Ink white cheesecloth and adhere to background. Tear and ink photo edges and mount. Stamp date onto mica piece and adhere to photo.

Jlyne Hanback, Biloxi, Mississippi

Supplies: Patterned paper (7 Gypsies); letter stamps (Hero Arts); white cardstock; cheesecloth; walnut ink; modeling paste; mica chip

True Hearts

An overlay title creates a dreamy effect for this layout. Begin with two purple cardstock backgrounds; mount section of leaf patterned paper vertically on right side of right page; embellish with leaf skeletons. Mat all photos on white cardstock and mount on pages. Print title and journaling on vellum cut to fit enlarged photo; mount over photo.

Lori Dickhaut, Sherwood Park, Alberta, Canada

Supplies: Leaf patterned paper (Autumn Leaves); leaf skeletons (Graphic Products Corp.); purple and white cardstocks; vellum

Jeffrey, I do not ask you to fulfill all my dreams; I only ask that you share them with me and allow me to share your dreams with you. I promise to do all in my power to keep our love as fresh and strong as it is today. I promise to be a true and loyal friend to you. I will try and be worthy of your love and trust. I will love you for today and for all of our tomorrows. From this day forward I will walk beside you. I offer you this ring as a symbol of my commitment and loyalty, as well as my enduring love for you.

Giving the Ring

A small album size doesn't impair the big impact of this stunning wedding spread. Begin with two 7 x 7" glossy black cardstock backgrounds. Double mat photo for left page on lilac and white glossy cardstocks; mount. Punch squares from glossy lilac cardstock; mount at center of right page, turning center square at an angle. Journal on vellum and mount on page over squares. Double mat silver embellishments and mount on bottom of page.

Aimee Houghton, Shreveport, Louisiana
Photos: W. Moriace Photography

Supplies: Glossy black, white and lilac cardstocks (Scrapbook Mania); silver embellishments (Card Connection); square punches

Now and Forever

Multiple products and papers support rather than overwhelm a photo of a stunning bride and her groom. Layer pieces of patterned papers on tan patterned paper background. Stamp various images and words and apply rub-on words arbitrarily on page. Mount photo using black photo corners. Adhere definition twill tape across center of page, stringing through ribbon charm. Embellish with raised "FOREVER" letters and decorative charm.

Julie Roanoke, Las Vegas, Nevada

Supplies: Patterned papers (7 Gypsies, Daisy D's, K & Company); image and letter stamps (Hero Arts, Inkadin-kado); definition twill tape (7 Gypsies); ribbon charm, word rub-ons (Making Memories); black raised letters (Wal-Mart); black photo corners; decorative charm

With This Ring...

Punched vellum flowers add a delicate touch to this starkly beautiful wedding page. Decoratively punch corners of black textured cardstock photo mats and mount photos, tucking photo corners into punched mat corners. Double mat photos on vellum and mount on black textured cardstock background. Mount torn vellum strip at bottom of page with sheer metallic ribbon. Write all text on vellum; tear out title, cut name/date block and mount both on background. Mat journaling on cardstock and adhere on sheer ribbon. Punch small and large daisies from vellum; layer to create flowers and embellish with beads. Triple mat on black cardstock and vellum and mount. Replace desired words in title with die-cut vellum letters mounted on black cardstock; affix over printed title words.

Dayna Gilbert, McMinnville, Oregon
Photos: Greg Jansen Photography, Minneapolis, Minnesota

Supplies: Black textured cardstock (Bazzill); decorative corner punches (Emagination Crafts); large daisy punch (Marvy); small daisy punch (EK Success); die-cut vellum letters (QuickKutz); vellum; sheer ribbon; clear beads

Le Memoire

Getting married on the same altar as your parents did 32 years before is an experience worthy of commemoration. Print photos on white cardstock; mount 1993 photo on red textured cardstock background. Cut section of preprinted transparency and mount on red cardstock background, overlapping mounted photo. Affix second photo on background atop transparency. Mat title cut from preprinted transparency on nickel luster cardstock; mount. Stamp dates and journal on strips of nickel luster cardstock; mount. Cover an image cut from preprinted transparency with epoxy cover and mount at bottom of page.

Marcy Mahar, Delmar, New York

Supplies: Red textured and nickel luster cardstocks (Bazzill); preprinted transparency, epoxy cover (Creative Imaginations); letter and number stamps (All Night Media); white cardstock; black ink

Cherish

The details of a special day are journaled on a page made to be cherished. Mat focal photo on purple textured cardstock. Mount on patterned paper background with metal photo corners. Create rub-on title on purple textured cardstock; double mat on patterned paper and purple textured cardstock and mount. Mat a strip of patterned paper on a strip of purple textured cardstock; mount and hang photo charm with fiber. Mat remaining photo on purple textured cardstock embellished with patterned paper strip; mount. Journal on white cardstock; mat on purple textured cardstock and mount.

Briana Fisher, Milford, Michigan

Supplies: Purple textured cardstock (Bazzill); patterned papers, rub-on word (Making Memories); metal photo corners, photo charm (Nunn Design); fiber; white cardstock

Coins, Cord and Veil

Special ceremony traditions are the focus of this special wedding page. Mat rectangular sections of green patterned paper and lime cardstock on purple and green textured cardstock blocks and mount both on purple patterned paper background. Journal onto cream cardstock; mat on black cardstock and mount with photos. Embellish page with silk flowers and acrylic stars. Cut title from cream and green textured cardstocks; mount. Stamp date.

Leah Blanco Williams, Kansas City, Missouri
Photos: Christa Hoffarth Photography, Omaha, Nebraska

Supplies: Green and purple patterned papers (Mustard Moon, Wordsworth); green and purple textured cardstocks (Bazzill); acrylic jewels (Hirschberg, Schutz & Co.); date stamp (Making Memories); silk flowers; green and cream cardstocks

Sand Ceremony

The powerful words spoken during a wedding ceremony drive this heavily journaled page. Chalk embossed paper piece and floral patterned paper background; adhere together. Journal on vellum, leaving space for photo to be mounted; adhere on page. Mat photo on white cardstock; mount. Apply word sticker on bottom of photo. Cut title from pink cardstock. Embellish page with acrylic jewels.

Leah Blanco Williams, Kansas City, Missouri
Photo: Christa Hoffarth Photography, Omaha, Nebraska

Supplies: Embossed and patterned papers (Magenta); word sticker (Bo-Bunny Press); acrylic jewels (Hirschberg, Schutz & Co.); chalk; vellum; white and pink cardstocks

With This Ring
I Thee Wed

A vellum overlay frame focuses the eye on the intimate moment witnessed in this wedding photo. Mount photo on white cardstock background. Cut frame opening from patterned vellum; adhere vellum overlay atop photo. Print title on clear vellum; crop and mount with brads.

Lisa Britchkow, Dresher, Pennsylvania
Photo: Tom Piazza Photography, Bensalem, Pennsylvania

Supplies: Patterned vellum (Autumn Leaves); white cardstock; clear vellum; brads

Why Do I Love You?

Decorative photo tags illustrate the sequence of events leading to final vows on this golden page. Begin by stamping pine cone image along bottom of patterned paper background. Sprinkle gold embossing powder on green textured cardstock and heat; tear and layer with torn gold textured paper on patterned paper background. Gold emboss heart brads; mount. Decoratively punch corners of three photos; mat on ivory textured cardstock blocks; gold leaf edges. Tie sheer ribbons through holes punched at top of mounted photos, mount with swirl clips. Print title and photo caption on torn green patterned paper; gold emboss before mounting. Attach caption on photo with swirl clip and embellish with additional clips.

Natalie Abbott, Lakewood, Colorado
Photos: Lee Bernhard of Colorado Classic Images, Colorado Springs, Colorado

Supplies: Pine cone stamp and heart brads (Creative Impressions); patterned papers and cardstocks (Crafter's Workshop); gold textured paper (Printworks); gold embossing powder; gold ink; sheer ribbon

The Moment Time Stood Still

A creative photo treatment makes this page a work of art. Distress photos using the method described below. Mat photos on black cardstock. Use photo-editing software to apply frame on enlarged focal photo; print and make copy on copy machine using regular photo copy paper and the "mirror" feature. Place photo copy facedown onto a piece of cardstock and rub over back of photo with photo transfer pen until all parts of the paper that you want transferred are saturated; peel paper away from cardstock. Mat with photo corners on black cardstock. Print title on vellum piece cut to fit one of the distressed photos; mount atop it with black photo corners. Adhere all photos and journaling onto patterned fabric trimmed to mat on black cardstock. Adhere ribbon below fabric when mounting on cardstock background stringing on heart charm. Secure charm to page. Cut clock from spare photo and mount on circle charm; adhere over clock on transferred photo.

Carrie O'Donnell, Newburyport, Massachusetts
Photos: Glenn Livermore Photography, Newburyport, Massachusetts

Supplies: Vintage photo distress ink (Ranger); The Print Shop (Broderbund); photo transfer pen (Impress Rubber Stamps); heart and circle charms (www.absolutelyeverything.com); patterned fabric; black cardstock; cotton ball; ribbon

1 To age and distress photos, use a sponge to heavily apply Vintage Photo Distress Ink directly to the picture. Use a cotton ball or soft cloth to gently wipe off excess ink. Allow to dry before mounting on your page.

Two Become One

A photo framed in sequins and layers of pretty papers takes center stage on this fetching layout. Begin by layering pink textured cardstock and white embossed paper on pink cardstock background; add layers of floral patterned paper, white embossed paper and green cardstock. Stitch edges of background page with floss. Draw large "X" in the middle of a sheet of double-sided paper; cut along lines and fold back sections. Mount atop photo. Adhere cut flaps to papers beneath. Journal on piece of double-sided paper; crop to triangle shape and mount on top of lower flap. Line edges of photo opening with sequins and jewels. Print title on white cardstock; mount on silver paper charm and then to page.

Nancy Korf, Portland, Oregon
Photo: Marie Martineau of Timeless Memories, Lacey, Washington

Supplies: Pink textured cardstock (Bazzill); patterned papers (Club Scrap, C-Thru Ruler); white embossed paper (K & Company); paper charm (Hot Off The Press); sequins; jewels; floss; white cardstock

For All Time

Digitally created background paper drives this compelling wedding layout. Crop and enhance selected photos. Open document in Photoshop Elements. Create background by enlarging focal photo and lowering opacity. Scan in page from dictionary; add atop photo to complete background. Colorize paper; add photos. Apply text using various fonts, shadows and bevels. Add tag using old time paper from Simply Vintage CD; add watch parts under journaling. Use Simply Vacations CD for the heart charm.

Michelle Shefveland, Sauk Rapids, Minnesota

Supplies: Photoshop Elements (Adobe); Simply Vintage and Simply Vacations CDs (www.CottageArts.net)

Now and Forever

A black-and-white palette creates consistence for this spread showcasing the fun and serious sides of the bridal couple. For left page, print title on white cardstock; cut into sections and chalk edges. Layer title strips, tulle and script patterned paper onto black cardstock background. Double mat photo on white cardstock and gray patterned paper; mount. Embellish with metal heart sticker. For right page, cut and chalk two white cardstock strips. Mount with script patterned paper on black cardstock background. Adhere double- and single-matted photos on page. Affix cropped photo on back of silver slide mount; embellish page with metal heart sticker. Wrap top of both pages with sheer ribbon; affix knotted tulle on top of ribbon and secure.

Lori Dickhaut, Sherwood Park, Alberta, Canada

Supplies: Script patterned paper (7 Gypsies); gray patterned paper (Masterpiece Studios); metal heart sticker (Magenta); slide mount; white and black cardstocks; charcoal chalk; tulle; ribbon

I Do

This wedding layout achieves a timeless look with inked papers. Use red and brown ink to add interest to a sheet of patterned paper. Trim and mount on black textured cardstock background. Mat photo on inked white cardstock. Adhere a strip of inked patterned paper on a textured black cardstock block; wrap sheer ribbon and buckle around right side. Mat on red striped patterned paper and mount. Mount matted photo on page. Stamp date on small inked tag; hang from buckle. Affix letter stickers on patterned paper strip. Attach metal "I DO" letters with brads. Stamp date randomly on background page.

Tracy Kuethe, Milford, Ohio

Supplies: Definition patterned paper, buckle (7 Gypsies); tag stamp (source unknown); black textured cardstock (Bazzill); red striped patterned paper (Pebbles); number stamps (All Night Media); letter stickers, metal letters, date stamp (Making Memories); red, brown and black inks; white cardstock; sheer ribbon; brads; small tag; floss

Happy Couple

Words and phrases are used to convey the special relationship between a husband and a wife on this dynamic page. Mount photo on top half of floral patterned paper background; adhere strips of sanded polka-dot paper and mauve textured cardstock on photo with brads. Journal on vellum and mount; affix strips of sanded polka-dot paper and cream textured cardstock across seams. Cut title from cream textured cardstock; chalk and mount. Use circle punch to cut mats from polka-dot paper for wooden title letters; mount wooden letters on punched circles and to page. Apply a silk flower and brad in the place of "o." Affix "Mr. & Mrs." tile and embellish page with brads, label, icicle letter and letter stickers for phrases.

Jennifer Bourgeault, Macomb Township, Michigan

Supplies: Floral and polka-dot patterned paper, mauve and cream textured cardstocks (Chatterbox); wooden letters (Li'l Davis Designs); silk flowers (Making Memories); tile (Junkitz); label sticker (Pebbles); icicle letter (KI Memories); letter stickers (Chatterbox, Creative Imaginations); brads; vellum

And The Greatest of These...

A peachy wedding day page reflects the special colors in a bride's bouquet. Print first names directly on bottom of cream textured cardstock background. Adhere torn peach paper piece across the center of the page. Tear section of peach patterned paper; crumple, sand and mount atop torn peach paper. Affix gold ribbon. Mat photo on peach paper and mount. Mount quote sticker. Adhere die-cut letters on bottom of page. Emboss skeleton leaf; mount. Ink flowers cut from cardstock; mount with buttons. Stamp date on small tag and hang from button.

Jennifer Sizemore, Woodbridge, Virginia

Supplies: Cream textured cardstock (Bazzill); patterned paper (EK Success); quote sticker (Daisy D's); die-cut letters (QuicKutz); skeleton leaf (Nature's Handmade Paper); date stamp (Making Memories); small tag (Avery); ruby embossing powder; peach paper; sandpaper; gold ribbon; buttons; amaretto ink

Our Wedding

A faux vintage photo is featured on this thoroughly modern colorful page. Cut patterned paper and yellow textured cardstock strips; cut patterned paper block. Treat all edges with brown ink and mount to light green background page. Mat photo on treated patterned paper block. Mount to background, leaving upper edge open for removable journaling tag. Journal on tag; ink edges and embellish with oval journaled die cut. String ribbon through holes in title die cut and adhere across bottom of page. Embellish with silk flowers.

Ruth De Fauw, Woodstock, Ontario, Canada

Supplies: Textured paper (Bazzill, Chatterbox); patterned paper (Chatterbox); oval tags; nails; ribbon; ink; silk flowers; flower tacks

A Gift

Catherine used an advertisement as inspiration for her powerful layout. Adhere section of embossed vellum on top half of patterned paper background. Sand edges of enlarged photo; mount on vellum piece. Adhere ribbon at bottom edge of photo. Journal on vellum; tear and mount. Punch tiny flowers and leaves from cardstock; compile and mount on journaling block and embellish with glitter glue. Mount photos on embossed vellum pieces. Cover right portions with torn printed vellum pieces. Cut diamond shapes from handmade paper to create ribbon holders. Fold diamonds over tag end; adhere, punch holes and tie ribbons and fibers through openings.

Catherine Crosby, South Jordan, Utah

Supplies: Patterned paper (Karen Foster Design); embossed vellum (Paper Adventures); flower and leaf punches (EK Success); handmade paper (Robert's Crafts); ribbon; vellum; fibers; glitter glue

Wedding

Knotted and bowed ribbon symbolizes the wedding knots tied by this couple on this celebratory page. Adhere blue cardstock on black textured cardstock background. Tear section of patterned paper and mount vertically on left side of page. Stitch around edge of entire page. Print word on transparency and mount. Punch holes for bows; string sheer ribbons through holes and tie. Print title on mauve textured cardstock mat; mount photo on top. Tear bottom and adhere strip of torn patterned paper on back; mount on page.

Dana Swords, Fredericksburg, Virginia

Supplies: Black and mauve textured cardstocks (Bazzill); patterned papers (Creative Imaginations, C-Thru Ruler); blue cardstock; transparency; sheer ribbons

Happiness

Stitching and metal embellishments add a unique look and feel to this united layout. Begin by layering strips of crackle patterned paper and black cardstock along bottom of green textured cardstock background; stitch along several edges. Stitch strip of yellow textured cardstock horizontally across page; apply rub-on title word. Stitch edges of cream cardstock mat for focal photo; wrap ribbons and attach charm. Mount photo behind ribbons and to page. Journal on cream cardstock; ink edges and adhere to page over strip of torn script patterned paper. Stitch floral patterned paper section at top of journaling. Ink edges of "marriage" definition sticker and mount. Embellish with metal framed photo.

Katherine Teague, New Westminster, British Columbia, Canada

Supplies: Crackle patterned paper (Karen Foster Design); green and yellow textured cardstocks (Bazzill); rub-on word, definition sticker, metal frame (Making Memories); ribbon charm (Jest Charming); script patterned paper (7 Gypsies); floral patterned paper (source unknown); ribbons; rose and black inks

Promise

A mini photo album makes it easy to display more photos on this compelling spread. Sand two patterned paper backgrounds; adhere sanded striped patterned papers on bottom of pages. Mount lace ribbon and beads across seams. On left page, stitch focal photo to background; adhere painted metal word. Mount smaller photos on both pages. Stitch patterned vellum cover on mini album; affix flower sticker. Wrap ribbon around mini album and stitch binding of album to right page. Use ribbon to close album. Apply rub-on words onto photos along bottom of pages.

Allison Kimball, Salt Lake City, Utah

Supplies: Patterned paper, flower sticker (K & Company); striped patterned paper, metal word, rub-on words, mini album (Making Memories); patterned vellum (source unknown); white paint; lace; strung beads; sandpaper; ribbon

Real Love Stories...

A 15-year-old wedding photo inspired this graphic layout. Begin by adhering sections of torn and cut patterned papers and handmade paper on black cardstock background. Mount printed border section on left side of page. Mat photo on red cardstock, inking edges. String gingham ribbons through ring and secure; mount photo. Affix strip of patterned paper on bottom of mat. Paint flower eyelets; sand. Set eyelets on mat and on border section. Affix word stickers on mat and border. Cut two sections of red cardstock for tag with one piece slightly shorter than the other. Mount decorative tag and saying sticker on shorter cardstock piece. Thread hinge on fiber and attach on both tags. Adhere tags together and mount.

Sue Fields, South Whitley, Indiana
Photo: Portraits By JoLene Hum, Huntington, Indiana

Supplies: Patterned papers (Bo-Bunny Press, Karen Foster Design, K & Company); word stickers (Bo-Bunny Press); handmade paper (Creative Imaginations); ring and hinge (7 Gypsies); black and red cardstocks; sandpaper; black ink; gingham ribbon; fiber

10-16-99

Torn paper rose petals frame a stunning black-and-white photo on this wedding page. Adhere photo on foam core board. Crumple, wet and flatten red cardstock; tear into petals. Layer petals on foam core board to frame photo and mount frame on patterned background paper. Print title on white cardstock; mount in circle tag, tie with raffia and mount tag to frame.

Heather Melzer, Yorkville, Illinois
Photo: Dianne Brogan Photography, Chicago, Illinois

Supplies: Patterned paper background (7 Gypsies); foam core board; red cardstock; circle tag; raffia

Love Forever

A collage of paper and stamped images creates a page that is timeless. Stamp large heart images on a torn sheet of definition patterned paper; layer additional stamped and inked sentiments on top. Mat photo on patterned paper; mount. Apply rub-on words as desired. Embellish page with tag stickers, word sticker, inked rickrack, stamped wood piece, index tab and epoxy sticker.

Sherrill Ghilardi Pierre, Maplewood, Minnesota
Photo: Peter Cmiel, Corcoran, Minnesota

Supplies: Patterned papers, definition patterned paper, index tab (7 Gypsies); gold embossed paper, epoxy sticker (K & Company); red patterned paper (Rusty Pickle); heart stamp (Close To My Heart); rub-on words (Making Memories); tag and word stickers (Creative Imaginations); letter stamps (Hero Arts); inked rickrack; wood piece; brads

Imagine a Love Eternal

A collage of love items creates a timeless wedding page. Create the background page by following the directions below. Tear out words from walnut-inked patterned paper and stitch on page. Stamp letters and words on stitched papers to create partial title. Stitch swirls and hearts to page. Double mat photo on mauve textured cardstock and patterned paper; mount. Embellish with decorative photo corners and aged eternal definition torn from dictionary to serve as part of title. Finish title with game tile letters. Tear out marriage definition; ink and stitch onto page. Embellish page with distressed vintage playing cards wrapped in fiber, silver key, measuring tape, heart charm and brad, safety pin, metal filigree, lace, torn and inked playing card paper, and stitched clock face. Tie ribbon onto metal hanger and sew hanger onto page. Layer definition sticker, printed transparency, and coin holder onto ribbons; knot ribbon ends and adhere woven label at bottom. Finish page with love definition, heart brad, strung beads, and framed transparency and sticker.

Andrea Lyn Vetten-Marley, Aurora, Colorado
Photo: Valerie Meadows of Meadows Photography, Boulder, Colorado

Supplies: Mauve textured cardstock (Bazzill); decorative brads, definition stickers (Making Memories); walnut-inked patterned paper, playing card patterned paper, printed transparencies (Design Originals); patterned paper, frame (K & Company); letter stamps (Hero Arts); eternal, marriage and love dictionary definitions (Funk And Wagnall's); key (EK Success); measuring tape (Prym Dritz); metal filigree (Halcraft); heart charm (source unknown); heart brad (Provo Craft); watch face (7 Gypsies); metal hanger and antique decorative photo corners (Crafts, Etc.); coin holder (source unknown); woven label (Me & My Big Ideas); brown cardstock; black and walnut inks; game tile letters; playing cards from vintage deck; fiber; safety pin; lace; ribbon

1 Create the decorative background by layering torn distressed mauve textured cardstock with brown cardstock on mauve textured cardstock background. Poke holes at even intervals around background edge. Use a running stitch to sew through holes. Repeat stitching until running stitch has formed a solid thread border.

2 Poke holes in selected pattern to create beaded embellishment. Pass threaded needle from underside of background to front side. Add beads before passing needle through next hole. Repeat until pattern is completed.

Pure Bliss

Michelle uses digitally created embellishments to make a beautiful digital wedding layout. Begin by opening tulip paper from Simply Elegant CD in Paint Shop Pro. Duplicate paper; change to desired color and tear bottom edge. Add atop tulip paper. Place photo on digital mat tearing right edge; place in background document. Use Simply Elegant CD to add all embellishments, vellum mat, text and tag.

Michelle Shefveland, Sauk Rapids, Minnesota

Supplies: Paint Shop Pro (Jasc); Simply Elegant CD (www.CottageArts.net)

Mr. and Mrs. McClung

Dimensional looking patterned paper helps make a quick and easy wedding layout. Mat photo on handmade embossed paper; mount matted photo on tan cardstock background. Stamp name on torn cream cardstock and emboss in gold; chalk and mount. Adorn with copper glitter, tulle, pearls and silk leaf. Embellish left side of page with frames, tulle, silk greenery and silk flowers.

Charlene McClung, Oceanside, California

Supplies: Handmade embossed paper (Jennifer Collection); patterned paper (Cloud 9 Design); letter stamps (Hero Arts); frames (Nunn Design); cream cardstock; chalk; copper glitter; tulle; silk flowers; pearls; gold embossing powder

Our Happy Day

A quilted frame atop a fabric background gives a homespun effect to the layout of this happy couple on their special day. Begin by sewing various fabrics onto black cardstock background. Next, adhere gold leaves on right side of page and stitch wide decorative ribbon on bottom. Create the frame by following the directions below. Print caption on green cardstock strip; mat on burgundy strip and adhere on page under photo. Stitch decorative cord pieces vertically onto page. Cut tag from faux paint sample and stamp bottom with rose image; sprinkle with gold embossing powder and heat to set. Dip edges of tag and mat cut for tag in embossing ink and emboss in gold; adhere together setting eyelet on top. Stamp title on tag using letter stamps and adorn with wire; mount on page.

Samantha Walker, Battle Ground, Washington
Photo: Sue Crockett, Rocklin, California

Supplies: Gold leaves (Graphic Products Corp.); rose image (Stampin' Up!); gold embossing powder; various fabrics (Carole Fabrics); black, burgundy and green cardstocks; wide decorative ribbon; sheer ribbon; mini brads; label holders; decorative cord pieces; faux paint sample; embossing ink; eyelet; black ink

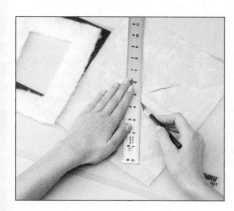

1 Create the decorative frame by cutting a cardstock frame and piece of batting to size. Cut a piece of fabric slightly larger than frame and batting. Cut a large "X" in the fabric's center.

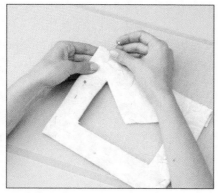

2 Wrap fabric around the frame and batting. Pin into place.

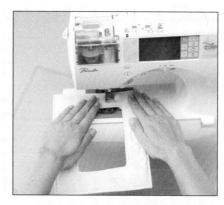

3 Stitch around the outside and inside edges of the frame. Stitch a quilting pattern by following designs on your fabric. Embellish with brads, sheer ribbon and label holder mounted over names and date. Mount on page atop photo.

You May Kiss the Bride...

Unforgettable

Lyrics from a song played at a reception supply the heartfelt journaling for this wedding page. Lightly print title directly on bottom of textured cardstock background; print lyrics on top of title. Mount section of patterned paper on background. Tear heart from textured cardstock, emboss with extra thick embossing powder; heat and crack when cooled. Chalk heart edges before hanging tag and mounting. Adhere photo.

Candi Gershon, Fishers, Indiana
Photos: Photography By Chez, Melbourne, Florida

Supplies: Textured cardstock (It Takes Two); patterned paper (K & Company); extra thick embossing powder (Ranger); chalk; small tag; fiber

After Those Vows...

A trinket book holds copies of this couple's wedding vows on this stunning page. Begin by inking patterned paper background edges. Using photo-editing software, add frame around photo and print. Adhere photo on cardstock; add metal photo corners and mount. Print tile and journaling on vellum; mount with black photo corners. Fill bracelet frames with tiny photos; secure sheer ribbon to ends of bracelet and adhere to top of layout.

Carrie O'Donnell, Newburyport, Massachusetts
Photo: Glenn Livermore Photography,
Newburyport, Massachusetts

Supplies: Patterned paper (Paper Loft); The Print Shop (Broderbund); metal photo corners, bracelet, tiny trinket book (www.absolutelyeverything.com); black ink; vellum; black photo corners; sheer ribbon; white cardstock

My Love

A romantic primary picture adds a dreamy feeling to this elaborate page. Use computer software to enlarge photo and change to black-and-white. Print on vellum and mount on white cardstock; adhere on patterned paper background. Print lyrics on vellum; chalk random words and mount. Affix ribbon vertically. Double mat photo on white and blue cardstocks; tear blue mat's bottom edge and apply pigment powder to tear. Write title on mat, tie sheer ribbon and mount. Mount photo onto mat with silver photo corners. Punch flowers and stems from green vellum and patterned paper; embellish with crystal stickers and layer on page. Cut page frame from blue cardstock; ink edges. Punch leaves and small flowers from vellum and adhere along frame. Cover with a layer of pigment powders and crystal lacquer; adhere frame to edges of page.

Catherine Crosby, South Jordan, Utah
Photo: Margo Moaremoff, Taylorsville, Utah

Supplies: Patterned paper (Karen Foster Design); flower, stem and leaf punches (EK Success); crystal stickers (Mark Richards Enterprises); small flower punch (Fiskars); pigment powder; crystal lacquer (Stampin' Up!); vellum; blue chalk; ribbon; white and blue cardstocks; black ink

Together Forever

This classically beautiful pastel layout is delicately embellished with fibers and buttons. Print journaling directly onto pink cardstock background. Mount torn piece of word patterned paper at bottom of page; layer torn floral paper on top, as well as at top of background page. String fibers through eyelets set in page corners. Affix title bubble words on fibers. Mount photo with black photo corners and embellish with heart charm and metal word accent. To make small sheer pouch, stitch edges of a folded piece of wide sheer ribbon. Fill with confetti and tie with silk ribbon before mounting. Embellish page with heart stickers and stitched buttons.

Sheri Reguly, Thunder Bay, Ontario, Canada

Supplies: Floral patterned paper (K & Company); word patterned paper (Creative Imaginations); bubble words (Li'l Davis Designs); heart charm (source unknown); metal word accent (DieCuts with a View); heart stickers (source unknown); black photo corners; pink cardstock; fibers; wide sheer ribbon; silk ribbon; confetti; buttons

Friends Love Always

Excellent wedding photos are the foundation of this starkly emotional wedding layout. Begin with two black cardstock backgrounds aligned side by side. Adhere flower photo and vertical black-and-white photo across both pages. Mount black-and-white photo on right page. Journal on transparency; adhere on right page. Mount small color photo on bottom corner of right page. Cut title from beige colored cardstock; mount on both pages. Cut portion from flower photo; adhere inside watch crystal and mount. Carefully cut along page seam to separate pages.

Renata Watt, Scoresby, Victoria, Australia

Supplies: Black and beige cardstocks; transparency; watch crystal

With a Kiss

A photo of the bride and groom's kiss and a pertinent quote keep this layout simple yet poignant. Print quote directly onto bottom of cream cardstock background. Adhere section of green patterned paper across center of page. Mount photo on black cardstock piece using clear photo corners and mount again onto page.

Karen Bukovan, Odessa, Florida

Supplies: Green patterned paper (Anna Griffin); black and cream cardstocks; clear photo corners

Giddy

A bride and groom's emotions are more than obvious in this layout created with Digital Image Pro. Open a new page and insert and manipulate and position photo. Grab one of the corner handles and drag it in so that the photo is slightly smaller than the page; center photo. Go to effect/edges/highlighted. Choose "thick under" to change the edge to black and the shape to a square; click done. Go to Insert/shape/square. Change the color to black and the line thickness to 0. Rotate it 45 degrees and then go to Format/resize object to fit canvas/stretch to fit. Move the diamond to the bottom of the stack. Go to insert/shape and choose the right triangle; fill it with black and make the line width 0. Move it to the corner and adjust the size so that it slightly touches the diamond. Hit CTRL/D three times, duplicating the triangle. Rotate and move them to their respective corners. Click on Insert text. Add text to lower right corner. Go to Effects/edges/highlighted/highlight over. Customize it by changing the highlight to white to finish.

Amanda Behrmann, Austin, Texas

Supplies: Digital Image Pro (Microsoft)

Kiss the Bride

A photo makes a stunning backdrop for this digital layout created in Photoshop. Enlarge a blurry photo to fill entire background. Adjust the hue/saturation levels to a saturation of -70 and adjust the hue to a soft sepia tone. Using the rectangular marquee tool, draw a box around the focal point and adjust the saturation to −100; give the box a black stroked line around it. In the lower left quadrant, create a box and use a Splat! filter from Alien Skin download to cut out a torn edged frame. Below this layer add photo behind the torn edged cut box. Used the fill stamp filter from Alien Skin to add the flower petals; adjust the hue/saturation levels to color as desired. Add additional flowers. To create the illusion of a falling photograph, add the photo to a separate layer; adjust the perspective transformation filter until it is the proper shape. Add highlights and shadow. Type title and add texture, bevels, shadows and pattern as desired.

Doris Castle, Fonda, New York
Photo: Carol Bluestein Photography,
Slingerlands, New York

Supplies: Photoshop (Adobe); Alien Skin download
(www.escrappers.com)

Forever

Elegance is often understated, as proven by this simple yet beautiful layout. Cut opening for photo from tan cardstock background; mount photo on backside. Apply mesh vertically down right side of page; affix slide stickers. Apply title on top of page with rub-on word.

Sara Bryans, Troy, New York

Supplies: Mesh (Magic Mesh); slide stickers and label holder (Memories Complete); rub-on words (Making Memories); tan and white cardstocks

Soul Mates

Realistic-looking beach paper and cut-outs capture an oceanside marriage ambiance. Mat photo on mulberry and mount on patterned paper background. Adhere cut-out words on left side of page with foam adhesive. Stamp title onto cut-out in gold; mount below photo. Affix twine below title; add metal embellishments.

Margert Ann Kruljac, Newnan, Georgia

Supplies: Patterned paper, cut-out words (NRN Designs); mulberry (Pulsar); letter stamps (All Night Media); metal embellishments (Prym Dritz); foam adhesive; gold ink; twine

Uo Iai Ka Manai Ho Okahi

A Hawaiian sunset creates the backdrop for this bride and groom's wedding kiss. Mat vellum sheet on blue textured cardstock background. Adhere tulle on bottom half of page. Stitch silver beads around page edge. Mount photo. Create frame from cardstock mounted on cardboard. Cover top half of frame in tulle. Cover entire frame with modeling paste. Mix sand with the paste on the frame's bottom half and create wavelike swirls in the frame's center. Paint dried paste white, then ink in shades of blue, adding pigment powder for shimmer. Cut title from cardstock; emboss letters and label holder white, adding pigment powder. Print journaling and date on yellow textured cardstock. Mount date on back of label holder and mount label holder on frame. Embellish label holder with thread and adhere frame over photo. Mount title. Tear out journaling and enhance edges with pigment powder; mount on similarly enhanced yellow textured cardstock piece. Create flower embellishments by punching and layering floral shapes. Paint with pigment powder and form while wet; add bead centers. For large flower in upper left corner, cover smaller flat flowers in tulle and mount dimensional flower atop them. Mount flowers.

Michelle Pendleton, Colorado Springs, Colorado
Photo: Rob Ratkowski, Pukalani, Hawaii

Supplies: Blue and yellow textured cardstocks (Bazzill); modeling paste (Liquitex); white paint (DecoArt); pigment powder (Ranger); flower punches (All Night Media, EK Success); vellum sheet; tulle; silver beads; various shades of blue ink; label holder; thread; beads; sand; white embossing powder

Cherish

A cinnamon palette and coordinating floral preprinted frames wrap this page in romance. Trim two beige patterned papers to mat on cinnamon colored cardstock backgrounds. Adhere sheer ribbon over gold spine and affix on page before adhering other ribbon pieces on pages. Mat all photos on white textured and non-textured cardstocks. Layer primary matted photo on preprinted frame; mat again on white cardstock and mount. Mount supporting photo on crumpled textured green cardstock leaving room to adhere "kiss" definition at bottom and mount. Adhere "promise" and "cherish" preprinted word blocks on crumpled cardstock and mount.

Heather Polacek, Niles, Ohio

Photos: Jacalyne Collier of Crown Image Photography, Hubbard, Ohio

Supplies: Beige patterned papers, preprinted paper elements (Cloud 9 Design); gold spine (7 Gypsies); white and green textured cardstocks (Bazzill); preprinted word blocks (Making Memories); sheer ribbon; white cardstock

And the Greatest of These Is Love

"Elegant" is the only word to describe this golden page. Mount patterned paper to burgundy cardstock background. Mat photo on burgundy cardstock and again on cream embossed paper mounted on second burgundy mat. Mount to background. Create vertical title embossing words on transparency set in burgundy cardstock frame. Embellish with rings and mount on background with self-adhesive foam spacers. Embellish with corner ribbon and buckle charm. Treat metal frame with gold leafing kit, following manufacturer's directions. Mount on page with journaling.

Denise Tucker, Versailles, Indiana

Supplies: Patterned paper (Creative Imaginations); embossed paper (Provo Craft); transparency; metal frame (source unknown); rings; gold leafing kit; extra thick embossing powder (Ranger); ribbon; self-adhesive foam spacers

Our Wedding Day

A heritage digital layout is created using Adobe Photoshop and scanned items. Begin with beige floral patterned paper scanned or downloaded. Duplicate it in green and move to top of page; add stitching. Add drop shadows for dimension. Repeat this stitching line on rectangle section at bottom of page. For journaling box, use a floral background on an oval shape adding a beige stroke around edge; add beige oval and text atop it along with the embossed fleur-de-lis embellishment. To make eyelets, create small circles cutting out the centers and using a filter to make them silver. Scan in gingham ribbon and apply to the tag, erasing where desired to give the "tied on" illusion. Scan in a piece of lace adding it to the top of the page and applying shadow. Create rectangles for photo mats; apply photos on top. Make photo corners with triangles colored beige; slightly darken the sides and add shadow. For title, scan in gold-rimmed buttons; color center black and add text. Scan in metal heart embellishment and accent with diamond downloaded from the Internet.

Ronna Penner, Waterloo, Ontario, Canada

Supplies: Photoshop (Adobe); gingham ribbon; lace; gold-rimmed button; metal heart embellishment

1st Official Kiss

A unique mosaic border on this page speaks to the romances that have blossomed throughout history. Mount cut slices of patterned paper side by side on right side of black cardstock background. Embellish with title created by stamping on clay tag embellished with wire and heart eyelet, letter beads and punch-out letters mounted beneath page pebbles. Adhere photo on page with silver photo corners. Cut "kiss" letters from photo embellishment blocks; adhere back into place and mount embellishment blocks on bottom of page.

Marpy Hayse, Katy, Texas

Supplies: Patterned paper, photo embellishments, clay tag, punch-out letters (ArtChix); letter stamps (Hero Arts, PSX Design); silver photo corners (Fiskars); lettering template (Scrap Pagerz); heart eyelet (Making Memories); letter beads (Impress Rubber Stamps): page pebbles (Magic Scraps); black cardstock; wire; brads

Must Be Love

A flower stamp on velvet creates an elegant backdrop for a loving wedding kiss. To create the velvet background, follow the directions below. Stitch top and bottom of stamped fabric to gold textured paper strips adhered to a cardstock background; add gold stitch lines across page. Tear photos, emboss edges in gold. Mount one embossed photo on black cardstock and line with gold pen; mount on page. Mat other photo on velvet striped paper; layer on torn gold paper and black cardstock. Journal on vellum strip and attach to photo with brads before journaling on backside of black cardstock. Use hinges to attach gold-matted photo to photo previously mounted on page; add metal embellishment. Emboss edges of black cardstock square in gold; write partial title on square and attach with brads. Cut remaining title from gold paper; emboss edges in gold and mount next to square. Write names and date on black cardstock; crop and mount on page under label holder.

Samantha Walker, Battle Ground, Washington
Photo: Mark Philbrick, Orem, Utah

Supplies: Glitter velvet (Jo-Ann Fabric); gold textured paper, velvet striped paper (FLAX art & design); watermark ink (Tsukineko); metal embellishment (Fancy Buckle Series); hinges; iron; black cardstock; gold and black pens; brads; label holder; gold embossing powder

1 To create the stamped background, place stamp facedown on glitter velvet.

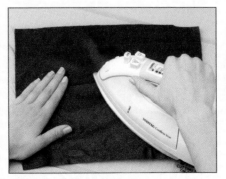

2 Flip velvet over and press an iron, set on medium heat, to the material overlaying the stamp. Repeat until desired design is achieved.

3 Allow material to cool before handling.

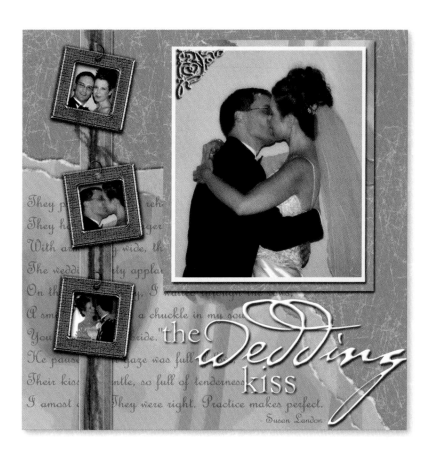

The Wedding Kiss

A pre-made template helped make the creation of this digital layout simple. Open the "Today We Walk" template from the Simply Elegant CD in Photoshop Elements. Change to desired colors. Add ribbon, fibers, frames and photo corner from the Simply Elegant CD. Add photos that have been enhanced in Paint Shop Pro and embossed text into document.

Michelle Shefveland, Sauk Rapids, Minnesota

Supplies: Photoshop Elements (Adobe); Simply Elegant CD (www.CottageArts.net) Paint Shop Pro (Jasc)

Kiss

A passionate photo is surrounded with creatively journaled kisses on this say-it-like-it-is page. Mat patterned paper at bottom and right sides of black textured cardstock background. Mat photo on yellow textured cardstock; mount. Print "kiss" in various fonts on transparency; add quote at bottom left corner and attach to page with flower eyelets. Cut title from white textured cardstock; mount.

Dana Swords, Fredericksburg, Virginia

Supplies: Patterned paper (Daisy D's); black, white and yellow textured cardstocks (Bazzill); flower eyelets (Making Memories); transparency

The Moment After I Do

Silk flowers create a pretty title border on this wedding layout. Mount square piece of blue cardstock to bottom corner of white textured cardstock background. Trim photos; double mat smaller photo on blue suede paper and torn, inked vellum. Mount both photos. Mount sections of personal letters above and below smaller photo. Affix silk flowers with bead centers across top of page. Stitch suede paper strips along edges of page elements. Apply suede die-cut title letters over flowers. Affix vellum envelope; insert torn, inked note. Embellish page with torn handkerchief, journaling pieces and beaded silk flowers.

Cori Dahmen, Portland, Oregon

Supplies: White textured cardstock (Bazzill); suede paper (K & Company); die-cut letters (QuicKutz); vellum envelope (Judikins); blue cardstock; white and blue inks; vellum; pearl beads; torn handkerchief; silk flowers

J&B Forever

Strong color choices and a strongly graphic layout are the backbone of this striking wedding page. Layer piece cut from purple textured cardstock with torn patterned paper piece onto black cardstock background. Affix ribbons at paper seams. Mat photo on white cardstock; mount. Ink definition sticker and mat on purple textured cardstock; mount. Stamp date on white cardstock scrap; mount with label holder and brads.

Katherine Teague, New Westminster, British Columbia, Canada

Supplies: Purple textured cardstock (Bazzill); patterned paper (7 Gypsies); letter stickers (Creative Imaginations); definition sticker, date stamp (Making Memories); black and white cardstocks; ribbons; black ink; label holder; brads

I'd Like to Present Mr. and Mrs....

Mr. And Mrs. Russell Fields

A simple layout maintains the focus on this stunning wedding photo. Cut sections of embossed and patterned papers; mount horizontally with foam adhesive on cream cardstock background. Triple mat photo on vellum, red cardstock and patterned paper; mount. Wrap sheer ribbon twice around top of page. Print title, place and date on cream cardstock; crop and mat on patterned paper. Affix decorative brackets on ends of title block and adhere on top of secured sheer ribbon.

Bethany Fields, Amarillo, Texas
Photo: Herb Crowell of Wagner's Studio, Amarillo, Texas

Supplies: Embossed and patterned papers (K & Company); decorative brackets (source unknown); foam adhesive; vellum; sheer ribbon

Mark & Heidi

A patterned vellum overlay supports formal wedding photos on this quick-to-create page. Mount photos on patterned paper background. Cut oval frame openings in embossed vellum and mount vellum atop photos; adhere floral stickers and floral corners. Mount quote sticker across bottom of page. Print names and date on sticker label; mount.

Heidi Kuester, Eau Claire, Wisconsin
Photos: T-BO Studios, Chippewa Falls, Wisconsin

Supplies: Patterned paper, floral stickers, floral photo corner stickers, label sticker (K & Company); quote sticker (Graffitti)

Amor Eterno

Create a stunning title frame with silk flowers for a blooming page. Begin by cutting window openings in foam core board, as described below. Treat foam core with crackle medium following manufacturer's directions. Embellish photo with tulle, charms, flowers and fibers. Mount photo on right side of cream cardstock background, aligning with previously cut window in foam core board. To create title, paint wooden letters with gold leafing pen and adhere on cream cardstock background, aligning with previously cut window in foam core board. Mount foam core board on top of cream cardstock background. Follow the directions below to embellish the title window opening.

Aida R. Franquiz, Auburndale, Massachusetts

Supplies: White textured cardstock (Bazzill); wooden letters (AC Moore); letter stamps (PSX Design); gold embossing powder (Stampin' Up!); concho (www.absolutelyeverything.com); charms (Boutique Trims); crackle, and white antique medium (Plaid); tulle; gold cord; silk flowers; foam core; small tag

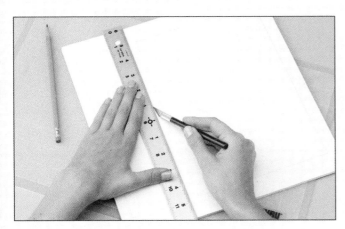

1 Use a ruler and pencil to mark off a window opening in a sheet of foam core. Cut opening using a craft knife.

2 Glue flowers into place along window edges, taking care to nestle each flower close against the one next to it.

Wedding Party

This page dedicated to friends and family is rich in both sentiment and color. Spray burgundy cardstock background with gold webbing. Mat focal photo on green cardstock; wrap sheer ribbon around bottom of mat and mount on page. Cut title from black cardstock; adhere on photo. Color heart die cuts with gold leafing pen; mount with green skeleton leaves and fiber-tied vellum tags. Adhere cropped photos on leaves and journal on tags. Cut journaling box from vellum and mount on bottom left corner under leaves; adorn with heart tag and photo. Journal on vellum.

Michelle Pesce, Arvada, Colorado
Photos: Eliot Khuner Photography, Berkeley, California;
Cheryl Pesce, Trabuco Canyon, California

Supplies: Gold webbing spray, gold leafing pen (Krylon); heart die cuts (source unknown); burgundy and black cardstocks; ribbon; fibers; vellum

Friendship Forever

A wedding commemorates a one-of-a-kind friendship between a man and woman, as honored on this lush page. Mount a wide and a narrow green velvet strip on patterned paper background; adhere thin strip of pink cardstock along seam of upper strip. Mount photo on page; cover with paper frame. Print quote on vellum; tear out into strips and mount before embellishing strip and page with sewn buttons. Mat one button on pink cardstock; mount and frame. Print partial title on vellum tag; tear bottom and affix on page with floral tag and button. Cut remaining title from white textured cardstock; mount on page.

Jennifer Bourgeault, Macomb Township, Michigan
Photo: Best Side Photo, Grosse Pointe Park, Michigan

Supplies: Patterned paper (Daisy D's); green velvet paper (Wintech); paper frame, floral tag (Cropper Hopper); white textured cardstock (Bazzill); pink cardstock; vellum; buttons; floss

Wedding Day

Candid moments are showcased in silver slide mounts, balancing out this enlarged formal bridal portrait. Mat blue patterned paper on blue cardstock background. Double mat photo on silver paper and blue cardstock, embossing cardstock edges in silver; mount. Mount photos on page beneath silver slide mounts. Adhere wedding day tag. Stamp date on torn vellum and attach on bottom of photo with brads.

Briana Fisher, Milford, Michigan
Photos: Jim Wildermuth of ArTech Photography Studio, Perry, Michigan

Supplies: Patterned paper (Daisy D's); silver paper (Paper Adventures); wedding day tag (EK Success); date stamp (Making Memories); silver embossing powder; blue cardstock; brads

Blissful

Simple lines and an intricately cut title contribute to this dainty layout. Mat mauve cardstock on green cardstock background. Mount photo on page. Cut narrow strips of green cardstock and mount across photo and mats in offset "T" shape. Cut title from mauve cardstock; mount on photo. Cut leaf and flower from green and mauve vellums; chalk and mount.

Renee Villalobos-Campa, Winnebago, Illinois
Photo: Mueller Studio, Rockford, Illinois

Supplies: Mauve and green cardstocks; green and mauve vellums; chalk

Love of a Lifetime

A lacy background and border act as a backdrop for this exquisite page featuring a spectacular photo transfer technique. In order to transfer "joined hands" photo onto fabric, follow the directions below. Cover trimmed cardstock piece with lace fabric; affix lacy trim on edge. Adhere piece on black textured cardstock background. Create triple mats for photos using black cardstock and silver paper; cover in tulle. Attach strung beads on corners of photos; adhere atop tulle-covered mats. Print names and date on vellum; mat on black cardstock and attach with decorative brads. Adorn page with dried roses and sheer ribbon tied in a bow.

Andrea Lyn Vetten-Marley, Aurora, Colorado
Photos: Kelli Noto, Centennial, Colorado

Supplies: Black textured cardstock (Bazzill); silver paper (DMD); fabric label and decorative brads (Making Memories); dried roses (Pressed Petals); lace fabric; lacy trim; tulle; beads; sequins; vellum; sheer ribbon

1 Create a photo transfer image of the "joined hands" photo. Brush on "Picture This" to cover the image. Make brush strokes on edges of the photo evident but try not to extend brush strokes to the white photo border area.

2 Place a piece of satin facedown on top of the painted image. Burnish with a burnishing tool.

3 Gently pull satin fabric from the photo.

Joy

A black background creates drama for this simple yet elegant layout that needs little embellishing. Adhere black fabric paper on black cardstock background. Using photo-editing software, apply frame on photo; print and mat on black cardstock. Layer onto page with decoratively cut lace paper. Mount spare photos on back of acrylic letters; cut out and apply crystal lacquer. Mount.

Carrie O'Donnell, Newburyport, Massachusetts
Photos: Glenn Livermore Photography, Newburyport, Massachusetts

Supplies: Black fabric paper, acrylic letters (www.absolutelyev-erything.com); The Print Shop (Broderbund); lace paper (Provo Craft); crystal lacquer (Judikins); black cardstock

Friends

Love is center stage on this muted spread featuring black-and-white photos. Tear two vertical strips from script patterned vellum and attach on ends of two pieces of striped patterned paper backgrounds using eyelets. On left page, mat focal photo on torn silver paper; mount. Wrap bottom of layout with fiber. Double mat metal word on black cardstock and torn silver paper; mount. Create adorned photo block by matting three smaller photos on black cardstock then to silver paper strip. Wrap ribbons between photos and embellish with punched flowers. Mat adorned photo block on black cardstock and then on page. For right page, mat photos on torn silver paper and mount on background. Adhere vellum "true love" sticker on torn black cardstock; mount. Punch flower from silver paper; attach on page with eyelet. Tie sheer ribbon on vellum tag; adhere die-cut heart and mount.

Nancy VandenBerghe, Dryden, Michigan

Supplies: Patterned vellum, vellum "true love" sticker, and vellum tag (EK Success); striped patterned paper (Masterpiece Studios); silver paper (Daler-Rowney); metal word (Making Memories); flower punch (Marvy); die-cut heart (QuicKutz); eyelets; fibers; black cardstock; sheer ribbon

Wonderful Warm Wedded Bliss

A combination of color photo and black-and-white photos gives this wedding page an unique perspective. Print title directly on upper part of green textured cardstock background; adhere section of handmade paper on bottom half. Mount cut strips of red cardstock on handmade paper piece; mount all photos on page. Cover title with metal frame.

Amy Workman, Langdon, Alberta, Canada
Photos: David Coates, Langdon, Alberta, Canada

Supplies: Handmade paper (Sunshine Papers); green textured cardstock (Bazzill); metal frame (Making Memories); red cardstock

Rain or Shine

A little rain can't stop a couple from having the wedding day of their dreams, and their upbeat photos carry the mood on this special spread! Begin with two green cardstock backgrounds. Mat all photos on white cardstock. Mount one matted photo in upper corner of left page and other in bottom corner of right page. Measure openings for vellum frames on both pages that allow room to reveal mounted photos. Print title and poems on vellum; cut out frames and mount over photos on both pages. Layer silk and sheer ribbon on pages; mount remaining matted photos.

Lori Dickhaut, Sherwood Park, Alberta, Canada

Supplies: Green and white cardstocks; vellum; silk and sheer ribbons

Love

Rectangular shapes supply continuity for this layout and support the vertically cropped photo. Mount various cut rectangle sections from green textured cardstocks on right side of light gold textured cardstock background; print journaling and draw black rectangle frame on background. Line edges of rectangles with gold leafing pen. Print photo with title, names and date at lower edge; mount. Adhere gold paper photo corners on photo. Cut hearts from light green textured cardstock, line with gold leafing pen and mount on page with foam adhesive. Hang gold heart charm from key chain; affix on page.

Sharon Whitehead, Vernon, British Columbia, Canada

Supplies: Light green, darker green and gold textured cardstocks; gold leafing pen; gold paper photo corners; gold heart charm (source unknown); key chain

Introducing Mr. & Mrs. John Linder

Dainty flowers punched from vellum and adorned with beaded centers create elegance on this layout. Double mat photo on black cardstock and large torn vellum block. Punch large and small daisies from vellum; layer, embellish with pearl beads and mount on mat. Create torn vellum border in the same manner. Print title on vellum; crop and mount.

Dayna Gilbert, McMinnville, Oregon
Photo: Greg Jansen Photography, Minneapolis, Minnesota

Supplies: Large daisy punch (Marvy); small daisy punch (EK Success); black cardstock; vellum; pearl beads

Love

A collaged background of wedding photos and creative embellishments make this layout something special. Arrange photos into a 12 x 12" collage. Scan and print photo collage onto white vellum then onto floral patterned paper. Scan in "Love" paper, eliminating those sections you do not wish to print; add original text. Print words onto adhesive-backed vellum; cut and apply in various locations. Create mini domino tiles by following the directions below. Attach chalked and stamped domino tiles to page. Mat photo on silver paper. Stamp the word "Love" into metal sheet; mount on slide mount. Shape ¹⁄₁₆" aluminum coil around slide mount and into heart shapes; hammer flat and adhere on tiles, page and slide mount. Create a journaling book behind the slide mount using photos on the top of the book that will show through the slide and embellish with beads. Mount metal word on bottom left corner of page; adhere heart charm atop second letter in word.

Jenny Moore Lowe, Lafayette, Colorado

Supplies: Floral patterned paper (Nancy Phelps); love page (Daisy D's); adhesive-backed vellum (ChartPak); silver paper; domino tiles; letter stamps (Hero Arts); metal stamps (source unknown); metal sheets (AMACO); slide mount; ¹⁄₁₆" aluminum coil (source unknown); metal word (Making Memories); photo-editing software; vellum sheets; chalk; transparency; beads; wire; heart charm; ink

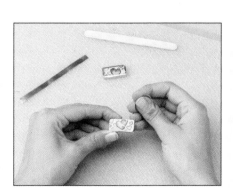

1 Create the tiny "LOVE" tiles with mini domino tiles. Apply yellow, pink then blue chalk randomly on back of tiles, covering the entire surface. Blend colors with cotton balls.

2 Ink mini heart stamps and stamp onto chalked tiles using solvent based ink. Allow tile to dry completely or use a heat gun to set.

3 Cut a square of clear transparency to fit the top of the tile. Wrap tile edges with silver flashing, attaching the transparency as you work. Smooth edges, corners and top of flashing with a wooden stick or burnishing tool.

Legacy of Love

This wedding page is a tribute to a love that lasted. Adhere cut, torn and chalked patterned paper sections on tan textured cardstock background. Chalk background page to age. Mount photo on page over red cardstock piece adhering on top and bottom edge of photo only to allow journaling tag to slip behind. Apply title with letter stickers. Embellish bottom right corner with paper and metal flower. Cut tag from patterned paper; adorn with metal word and gingham ribbon. Journal on tag and slip behind photo.

Kari Barrera, Warrenton, Virginia

Supplies: Patterned papers (Anna Griffin, Provo Craft, 7 Gypsies); tan textured cardstock (Bazzill); letter stickers (Creative Imaginations); paper and metal flower (source unknown); metal word (Making Memories); gingham ribbon

Once in a Lifetime...

A pretty foam core frame gives this loving layout great dimension. Tear strips of black cardstock and gold patterned paper; layer onto tan fabric patterned paper background to form page border. Crumple, wet and open up patterned paper to create mat; mount photo on mat and mount on page. Cut black foam core frame and wrap with wire. Embellish with silk flowers adorned with glitter glue. Print title on patterned paper; crop in decorative shape and adhere on frame.

Holle Wiktorek, Reunion, Colorado
Photo: Narcissus Magturo of NAM Photography, Ft. Leonard Wood, Missouri

Supplies: Gold and tan fabric patterned papers (Anna Griffin); silk flowers; glitter glue; black cardstock; black foam core; wire

For All Eternity

Faith is the backbone of this couple's love, as presented on this periwinkle blue layout. Mount strips of patterned vellum on bottom of two patterned paper backgrounds. Mat cropped photos on torn mulberry and mount on pages. Cut three small rectangles from patterned vellum; embellish with punched flowers, stems and ribbon bows. Print caption on one of the squares and embellish with watch pieces. Enhance flowers with gel pens, crystal lacquer and glitter glue. Mat larger photos on patterned vellum; adhere patterned vellum piece over photo of church. Mount silver cardstock photo corners on all photos and vellum squares. On left page, layer vellum-covered photo, matted photo, sheer ribbon and torn mulberry onto patterned paper background; tie ribbon bow. Adhere photos on right page on mulberry then onto background. Embellish page corners with punched flower bouquets.

Catherine Crosby, South Jordan, Utah
Photos: Margo Moaremoff, Taylorsville, Utah

Supplies: Patterned vellum, mulberry paper (source unknown); patterned paper (Karen Foster Design); flower and stem punches (EK Success); crystal lacquer; glitter glue; gel pens; silver cardstock; clock parts; sheer ribbon

Moving Moments

Photo manipulation software creates an embossed looked on this moving spread. Choose photo for background; mirror the image and distort using the glass filter. Create frame around flowers on left and couple on right; emboss edges. Place other photos on background and create frame with outer glow for a matting effect. Apply shadow text on background; emboss the title portion of the journaling.

Lori Dickhaut, Sherwood Park, Alberta, Canada

Supplies: Photoshop (Adobe)

Daughter-in-Law

A groom's parents grace the photos in this wedding page honoring a new family connection. Begin by mounting purple inked sections of patterned paper and coordinating geometric shapes on tan speckled cardstock background. Mount photos. Cut title from ivory cardstock; adhere on page right and left. Cut tag from green cardstock and mount; adorn with acrylic flower and rickrack. Print quote on vellum; mount across photo and tag. Apply letter stickers on tag.

Leah Blanco Williams, Kansas City, Missouri
Photos: Christa Hoffarth Photography, Omaha, Nebraska

Supplies: Patterned paper and coordinating geometric shapes (Kopp Design); tan speckled cardstock (Bazzill); acrylic flower (www.memoriesoftherabbit.com); letter stickers (Bo-Bunny Press); purple ink; ivory and green cardstocks; rickrack; vellum

Lucas and Kristi
August 23, 2003

this day i thee wed

This Day I Thee Wed

Pearl beads decorate this bridal page just as they decorate the bride's gown. Cut section from flower embossed paper. Stitch pearl beads strategically on floral embossed paper. Mount beaded embossed section on slate cardstock background. Mat enlarged photo on white cardstock; mount on page with unmatted photo overlapping them. Adorn left corners of large photo with metal decorative corners. Print names and date on white cardstock; affix on page under silver frame. Cut strip from blue cardstock for border strip; cover with tulle, securing on back. Affix beaded trim along top and bottom edge of border. Adhere border on bottom of page. Apply title with rub-on word.

Diana Hudson, Bakersfield, California
Photo: Kelli Noto, Centennial, Colorado

Supplies: Flower embossed paper (Jennifer Collection); metal decorative corners (Boutique Trims); silver frame (source unknown); rub-on word (Making Memories); slate, white and blue cardstocks; tulle; pearl strand; pearl beads

Take My Hand

A poem written by the groom serves as inspiration for this layout. Tear section from the middle of green cardstock; roll torn edges and mount on ivory patterned paper background. Stitch along bottom of rolled edge; affix flower stickers and beads. Mat photo on torn green cardstock mat; roll edges, add silk flowers in corners and mount. Print title on patterned paper; tear top edge and mat on torn green cardstock. Tear hole in upper part of mat; roll edges, stitch below, and adhere patterned paper piece on back. Affix flower sticker and beads in heart shape; mount.

Wendy Malichio, Bethel, Connecticut

Supplies: Patterned paper (Anna Griffin); flower stickers (EK Success); silk flowers; green cardstock; beads

Happily Ever After

A photo with a unique perspective becomes the focus of this energetic page. Sew floral patterned paper on the left side of gray textured cardstock; adhere striped patterned paper block on right. Mount photo; apply rub-on word title. Embellish with lace ribbon, pink silk flowers and brads. Journal on vellum; mount with metal accent. Mount smaller photo on metal tag and attach to page.

Patricia Anderson, Selah, Washington
Photos: Yuen Lui, Seattle, Washington

Supplies: Patterned paper, gray textured cardstock, striped patterned paper (Chatterbox); rub-on word (Making Memories); metal accent (Boutique Trims); lace ribbon; pink silk flowers; brads; vellum; metal tag

Join Us for A Celebration!

I Am Married To My Best Friend

The title says it on this happy-go-lucky page, but the great photo just reinforces it! Mount photo on dark purple textured cardstock background. Adhere mesh strip, thin strips of green textured cardstock and strip of light purple textured cardstock vertically on right side of page. Print words on dark purple and green textured cardstocks and cut into circles. Tie gingham ribbon through eyelet set in largest circle; mount brads on smaller circle, adhere brads with "love" rub-on letters. Cut extra circles of varied sizes from cardstocks; line edges with silver leafing pen and mount. Apply title stickers, metal letter and metal words to page; ink one of the words in black. Adhere heart plaque on bottom of page; mount brads decorated with rub-on letters. Cover desired letters with page pebbles.

Sharon Whitehead, Vernon, British Columbia, Canada

Supplies: Dark, light purple and green textured cardstocks (Bazzill); mesh (Magic Mesh); silver leafing pen (Krylon); brads, rub-ons (Creative Imaginations); letter stickers (Wordsworth); metal letters, metal words, plaque, page pebbles (Making Memories); eyelet; gingham ribbons; brads; colored brads; black ink

Traditions

A layout featuring nontraditional photos in which the bride's face is never seen is compelling in its mystery. Mount cut sections of floral and plaid patterned papers and green textured cardstock on purple textured cardstock background. Bend top right corner of paper over and attach with clear nail. Mount photos. Apply title rub-on word. Mount ribbon and charm at bottom of page.

Erin Sweeney, Twinsburg, Ohio

Supplies: Floral and plaid patterned papers, green and purple textured cardstocks, clear nail (Chatterbox); rub-on title word, ribbon charm (Making Memories); ribbon

Facing The Future

Funny-faced mugs make this fun-lovin' page especially lively. Adhere title printed on vellum section to purple patterned paper background. Attach floral lace ribbon embellished with beaded flowers and pearls. Mount section of scroll patterned paper at bottom right corner of page. Double mat photos on vellum and green handmade paper; tear and mount. Print name and date on vellum section; mount. Enlarge and silhouette cut goblet images printed on cardstock. Mount on textured cardstock and trim to fit. Fold to form booklet. Create photo story pages and mount inside booklet. Adorn goblets with wine charms. Mount booklet on torn green handmade paper and mount on page. Embellish with goblets cut from purple suede paper.

Jenny Moore Lowe, Canon City, Colorado
Photos: Owens Photography

Supplies: Purple patterned paper (Crafts, Etc.); green handmade paper, suede paper (K & Company); scroll patterned paper (Making Memories); Photoshop (Adobe); gray textured cardstock (Bazzill); vellum; floral lace ribbon; beads; pearls

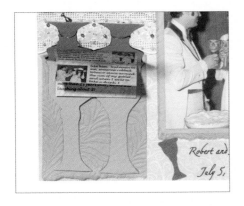

Wishes For Us

Journaling detailing wedding traditions that were not captured in photos makes this spread unique. Mount large section of green textured cardstock on white textured cardstock background. Cut two thin strips from green textured cardstock and two shorter pieces from green suede paper. Paint decorative brads with acrylic paint and attach at ends of strips. Mat photos on green suede paper and adhere on textured cardstock section. Print journaling on vellum cropped the same size as matted photo; affix atop photo. Mount die-cut suede title letters.

Cori Dahmen, Portland, Oregon

Supplies: Green and white textured cardstocks (Bazzill); green suede paper (K & Company); decorative brads (Making Memories); die-cut suede title letters (QuicKutz); vellum

A Toast

A painted canvas frame and flowers add to this bride's pretty-in-pink moment. Cut handmade paper into two strips with one being narrower than the other; line edges with gold leafing pen and mount on pink cardstock background. Adhere lace between handmade paper strips. Paint paper flowers with acrylic paint and mount on lace. Cut partial title from cardstock; gold leaf and mount on lace. Finish title by writing letter "A" with gold leafing pen on metal-rimmed vellum tag. Mount tag, tucking under lace. Line photo in gold; mount. Paint canvas frame and line edges in gold. Wrap top and bottom with lace; adorn with painted flower and gold enhanced metal letters. Adhere over photo on page. Print journaling on pink textured cardstock; mount.

Shannon Taylor, Bristol, Tennessee

Supplies: Handmade paper (Artistic Scrapper); gold leafing pen (Krylon); paper flowers (Natural Paper Co.); lettering template (Chatterbox); canvas frame (Li'l Davis Designs); metal letters (Making Memories); pink textured cardstock (Bazzill); pink cardstock; lace; vellum tag; acrylic paint

Laughter

A humorous spontaneous moment is captured on film and showcased in this lighthearted layout. Affix border sticker on right side of peach cardstock background. Mat photo on patterned paper and attach photo corner stickers. Double mat on coordinating patterned paper and apply decorative border to lower edge before mounting. Print title and journaling on torn vellum; string title with fiber. Mount journaling on page. Emboss slide mounts in gold and layer over vellum and rose buttons; add photo corner stickers. Attach to page at ends of fiber.

Shannon LeBlanc, Kenner, Louisiana

Supplies: Border sticker, photo corner stickers, patterned papers (K & Company); slide mounts (Jest Charming); rose buttons (Jesse James); peach cardstock; fiber; vellum; gold embossing powder

Wedding Toasts

A pretty documentation of the wedding toast is captured on this wedding scrapbook page. Trim striped patterned paper to mat on black cardstock background; sand edges and mount. Crop main photos into squares; adhere on piece of sanded pink cardstock and mount on center of page over torn floral vellum piece. Mat light pink cardstock strip on sanded pink cardstock for lower page border. To create the floral border strip, follow the directions below. Embellish black metal-rimmed tags with silk flowers, a button, champagne tile and brad. Mount on bottom border piece. Sand edge of pink cardstock strip; mount across top of page. Mount cropped photo on strip. Use letter stickers, wooden letter, icicle letter and handcut word for title; adhere on page. Journal on upper corner of torn vellum; attach at top corner of page with stitched buttons.

Jennifer Bourgeault, Macomb Township, Michigan
Photos: Best Side Photo, Grosse Pointe Park, Michigan

Supplies: Striped patterned paper, floral vellum (Chatterbox); flower stamp (source unknown); black metal-rimmed tags, silk flowers (Making Memories); champagne tile (Junkitz); letter stickers (Creative Imaginations, Me & My Big Ideas); wooden letter (Li'l Davis Designs); acrylic letter (KI Memories); clear embossing powder; black, pink and light pink cardstocks; sandpaper; white ink; buttons; fiber; brads

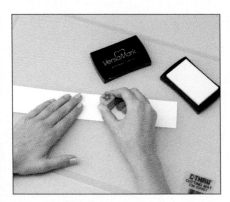

1 Create the floral border strip by stamping a flower image with watermark ink.

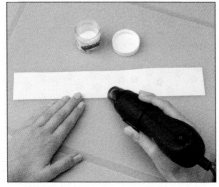

2 Sprinkle clear embossing powder over watermark ink stamped images and heat with a heat gun to set.

3 Use a makeup sponge of finger dauber to dab pink ink over the entire border to create highlighted effect. Adhere border horizontally across previously mounted pink border strip.

Sweets for My Sweetheart

A frothy iced wedding cake lends its texture to this lighter-than-cream wedding page. Sew floral fabric pieces on purple cardstock background. Lace ribbon with rings through small eyelets at bottom right page corner. Quadruple mat focal photo on white and purple cardstocks; adhere silk flowers on corners and mount. Double mat remaining photos and stitch to page. Print title on torn vellum; chalk edges, mat on mulberry and mount with brads. Print names and dates on cardstock; mount on page under label holders. Set large eyelets in corners of page; create tulle border by pulling through eyelets. Emboss vellum cake image using stencil; add bead embellishment. Top cake with flower stickers and stitch to page.

Andrea Lyn Vetten-Marley, Aurora, Colorado

Supplies: Silk flowers (Offray); mulberry paper (Pulsar); wedding cake stencil (Fiskars); flower stickers (EK Success); fabric; purple and white cardstocks; eyelets, ribbon; wedding rings; vellum; chalk; brads; label holders

It's So Much More...

Meaningful journaling carries this spread that is weighty in embossed papers and embellishments. Colorize embossed papers with purple metallic rub-ons; trim and mount on purple cardstock backgrounds. Print title, photo captions and journaling on white cardstock; cut out and colorize edges with purple rub-ons. Tie fibers on tag title. Mat large journaling box on purple cardstock; tie fibers through punched holes, attaching painted charm. Create modeling paste mats by mixing the paste with red and blue food coloring; smear onto heavyweight cardstock. While wet, emboss designs with toothpick. Mat all photos on white cardstock then mount on dried modeling paste mats; mount on both pages. Adhere captions onto photos using label holders, and journaling on pages with foam adhesive. Embellish with painted and colorized metal hearts and ribbon.

Denise Tucker, Versailles, Indiana

Supplies: Embossed paper (Provo Craft); purple metallic rub-ons (Craf-T); embossing paste (Dreamweaver Stencils); ribbon holder (Making Memories); purple and white cardstocks; fibers; white acrylic paint; foam adhesive; label holders; food coloring; ribbon

Wedding Cake

A cake big enough for everyone to share is show-cased on this sweet but simple wedding page. Layer torn vellum sheet and green patterned paper on floral patterned paper background. Enlarge cake photo and mat on green cardstock; mount on page. Mat smaller photo on patterned paper; adhere bow on bottom and affix to page. Journal on green cardstock; mount.

Kim Fleming, Dumfries, Virginia
Photos: Thomas Van Veen Photography,
Bethesda, Maryland

Supplies: Vellum; green and floral patterned papers (Anna Griffin); green cardstock; bow

Cake Cut

A glimmer of tin provides a glow for this unique wedding page. Paint tin background tile with pearl champagne paint and highlight the raised areas with silver metallic rub-ons. Mount photo on tin background. Trim with satin ribbon and pearls; add decorative photo corners. Trim tin background edge with rhinestone chain. Paint wedding cake accent to match tin. Treat word charm with paint and rub-ons to coordinate and mount on page.

Jeniece Higgins, Lake Forest, Illinois

Supplies: Tin background (Artistic Expressions); eyelet letter and charm (Making Memories); ribbon; pearls; rhinestone chain; wedding cake accent (flea market); paint; silver rub-ons; transparency

Oh, My Love...

A restored photo that was damaged in a flood 20 years earlier is featured on this stunning page. Print title on embossed paper; mount on cardstock background. Wrap sheer ribbon around top of page; embellish ribbon and page with heart swirl clips. Print song lyrics on cream cardstock; mat on green cardstock and mount with brads. Mount photo; embellish corners with heart swirl clips and brads.

Marianne Dobbs, Alpena, Michigan
Lyrics: Righteous Brothers

Supplies: Embossed paper (Club Scrap); heart swirl clips (Making Memories); green and cream cardstocks; brads

May I Have This Dance?

A stolen moment alone creates an intimate mood for this lush page. Layer textured green cardstock and patterned paper on black textured cardstock background. Mount photo. Print date at top, "first dance" at bottom, and journaling in the middle of cream cardstock strip, leaving out the first letter. Cut missing letter from green textured cardstock and adhere in place. Attach ribbons, lace and fabric label to page with safety pins.

Joanna Bolick, Fletcher, North Carolina
Photo: Leon Bolick, Charlotte, North Carolina

Supplies: Black and green textured cardstocks (Bazzill); patterned paper (Chatterbox); fabric label (Me & My Big Ideas); ribbon and safety pins (Making Memories); cream cardstock; lace

Forever

An altered tin holds the story of a bride and groom, and tags open to display mini photos and embellishments on this complex, but can-do spread. Begin with two pieces each of black cardstock and foam core board. Mat focal photo for left page on metallic paper and then on black cardstock background. Mount smaller photo on right page on top of bowed ribbon segment. Cover foam core boards with cut and torn pieces of patterned papers and cream cardstock; ink edges. Cut frame openings from foam core to reveal photos on background pages below and for altered tin window; adhere backgrounds onto boards. Pull bow and ribbon up through frame opening onto board; adhere decorative frame. Create tags for left page with patterned papers; fold bottom half upward to close. Mat small tag photos, metal plaque and journaling blocks on patterned paper; adhere on tags. Sew buttons on tags; attach brad heads and string for latching. Ink and sand label holders; attach over names on left page. Stamp initial on torn paper; embellish with buttons and brads before mounting at bottom of left page. Decorate tin with patterned papers, silk flowers, ribbon, buttons, brads and altered label holder. Place desired items inside tin. Mount onto right background over ribbon piece. Place metal "forever" word inside sheer bag; mount on top of right page.

April Geer, East Hartford, Connecticut
Photos: Carol Klein, Tolland, Connecticut

Supplies: Patterned papers (7 Gypsies, Anna Griffin); metallic paper (The Paper Cut); clear photo corners (3L); bow and ribbon (Anna Griffin); decorative frame, metal plaque and word (Making Memories); letter stamp (Santa Rosa); black and cream cardstocks; black ink; foam core boards; clear photo corners; buttons; brads; label holders; silk flowers; ribbons; sheer bag

Now and Forever

A love deep enough to last forever is commemorated on this intricate page. Cut section from black patterned paper and mount on bottom of tan patterned paper background; affix gingham ribbon. Mount metal phrase plaque on ribbon. Adhere torn red cardstock section vertically on left side of page. Mount smaller photos on red cardstock section. Mat focal photo on black cardstock and mount. Apply rub-on title. Journal on vellum; tear bottom edge and mat on red cardstock. Mount on bottom of page with eyelets. Embellish distressed tag with torn script patterned paper and cardstock heart; embellish with lace trim, hemp cord, beads and patterned paper covered metal-rimmed tag. Tie tag with fuzzy fibers and mount.

Cindy Johnson-Bentley, Allen, Texas

Supplies: Black patterned paper, script patterned paper (7 Gypsies); tan patterned paper (Creative Imaginations); metal phrase plaque, rub-on words (Making Memories); red gingham ribbon; red and black cardstocks; vellum; eyelets; distressed tag; lace trim; hemp cord; beads; patterned-paper-covered metal-rimmed tag; fuzzy fibers

Come Rain or Shine

Aged photos and a distressed cardboard background create a rustic look for this page. Adorn section of dictionary patterned paper with gold photo corners; layer with aged photo, stamped envelope and black corrugated paper. Embellish with gingham ribbon, gold bar and quote; mount piece on cardboard background. Journal on vellum piece cut to fit photo; attach on photo with eyelet and mount on cardboard background. Set eyelet in corner of smaller aged photo; embellish with spiral clip and mount.

Jennifer Bertsch, Tallahassee, Florida

Supplies: Dictionary patterned paper, gold bar, spiral clip (7 Gypsies); gold photo corners (Nunn Design); black corrugated paper (DMD); letter stamps (Hero Arts); distressed cardboard background; envelope; gingham ribbon; vellum; eyelets; black ink

Love Always Trusts

A preprinted transparency makes a meaningful overlay on this quick and easy page. Begin by mounting section cut from floral patterned paper on right side of script patterned paper background. Attach preprinted transparency atop page; wrap gingham ribbon and embellish it with buttons and embossed stickers mounted with foam adhesive. Adhere cropped photos on stitched patterned paper piece; double mat on sage and burgundy cardstocks and mount. Affix embossed floral sticker on stitched-looking patterned paper piece; double mat same as photo and mount.

Melanie Cantrell, Olathe, Kansas

Supplies: Floral, script and stitched-looking patterned paper, embossed stickers (K & Company); preprinted transparency (Creative Imaginations); gingham ribbon; buttons; foam adhesive; burgundy and sage cardstocks

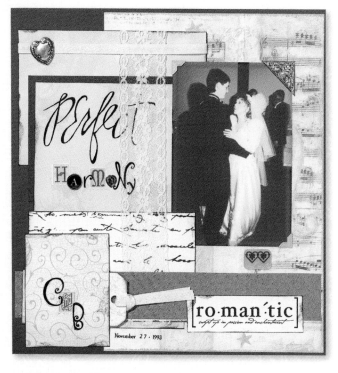

Perfect Harmony

A pull-out tag offers additional journaling space on this altered-looking wedding page. Begin by layering cut and inked sections of various patterned papers, metallic copper paper, lace ribbon, silk ribbon and brown textured cardstock onto brown cardstock background. Mount sepia-printed photo on page using tan and pewter photo corners. Affix poem stone below photo. Create title with letter stickers and a rub-on word. Ink section of patterned paper and adhere top and bottom edges to background to allow journaling tag to slip behind; embellish with letter stickers. Journal on inked tag; tie silk ribbon and slip behind paper piece. Stamp date on bottom of page.

Brandi Barnes, Kelso, Tennessee

Supplies: Various patterned papers (7 Gypsies, Frances Meyer, Provo Craft); metallic copper paper (Hobby Lobby); brown textured cardstock (Bazzill); Microsoft Picture It! (Microsoft); pewter photo corner (Magenta); rub-on word, date stamp (Making Memories); letter stickers (Creative Imaginations, EK Success); poem stone (Creative Imaginations); brown cardstock; lace and silk ribbons; tan photo corners

The Details

The beautiful details of this bride's wedding dress are re-created with sequined trim on this floral page. Begin by printing title directly onto top of rose patterned paper background. Mount photo. Mount pink metallic ribbon across page; top with sequined rose trim.

Sharon Bissett O'Neal, Lee's Summit, Missouri

Supplies: Rose patterned paper (Masterpiece Studios); metallic pink ribbon; sequined rose trim

Rest in Me

A variety of software was used to create this digital layout. Open photo in Paint Shop Pro; alter as desired. Open document in Photoshop Elements; add scroll paper for background from Simply Vintage CD. Add photo mat from Simply Elegant CD; add photo. For fiber and heart charm, drag and drop onto document from Simply Elegant CD. Embellish document with torn vellum piece, doily and text from the same CD.

Michelle Shefveland, Sauk Rapids, Minnesota

Supplies: Paint Shop Pro (Jasc); Photoshop Elements (Adobe); Simply Vintage and Simply Elegant CDs (www.CottageArts.net)

Divide Labor

A metal journaling block and metallic webbing create consistency for this celebratory layout. Begin by wrapping copper wire strands around a pink cardstock piece trimmed to mat on dark pink cardstock background; secure on back and mount atop background. Stamp various images on dark purple cardstock; sprinkle with clear embossing powder and heat to set. Cut double frame from both pink and stamped cardstocks, leaving image at bottom right corner. Mount onto page over photo. Affix copper wire along frame edge. To create the metal journaling plate, see directions below. Print title on pink cardstock; cover with stamped image and dust with copper colored pigment powders. Double mat on dark pink cardstock and metal sheet; mount on top of page at frame corner. Repeat for stamped image on bottom right corner of frame, this time framing image with copper-wire covered frame.

Bay Loftis, Philadelphia, Tennessee

Supplies: Various stamps (Club Scrap); clear embossing powder, pigment powders (Ranger); embossable metal (AMACO); pink and dark pink cardstocks; copper wire; black non-smear pen

1 Create the metal journaling plate with an old-fashioned typewriter. Insert a thin copper metal sheet in a typewriter and carefully type your message. Cover typed letters with black non-smear pen and mount on page.

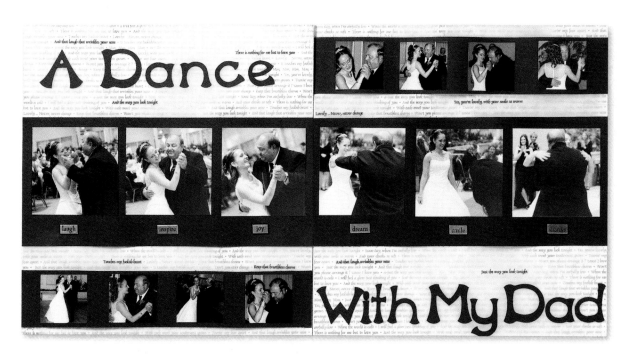

A Dance With My Dad

A special dance with Dad is as timeless as the love a daughter has for this first-ever man in her life. Print song lyrics on white cardstock pages. Print select lyrics on vellum; cut out. Mount vellum sheets on printed background pages; apply vellum lyrics in strategic places on vellum sheets. Adhere cropped photos on black cardstock sections; mount. Attach eyelet words below black-and-white photos. Cut title from black cardstock and mount.

Niki Magee, Florham Park, New Jersey
Photos: Manning Photography, Milwaukee, Wisconsin

Supplies: Eyelet words (Making Memories); lettering stencil (Provo Craft); white and black cardstock; vellum sheets

Everything I Do

Lyrics from a song that accompanied this bride and groom's first dance act as journaling for this emotional layout. Mount a cropped cream cardstock piece on black cardstock background. Mount photo on background; embellish with fiber. Print lyrics on torn vellum; chalk edges and mount with brads. String paper ribbon through holes on bottom corners of page; secure.

Angela Marvel, Puyallup, Washington
Photo: Valarie Dornoff, Federal Way, Washington
Lyrics: Bryan Adams

Supplies: Cream and black cardstocks; fiber; vellum; chalk; brads; paper ribbons

And They Lived Happily Ever After

This action filled page captures both the eye and emotion. Print title on bottom of a sheet of pink textured cardstock; mount on larger piece of black textured cardstock background. Wrap gingham ribbon around bottom of page and tie in a bow. Print black-and-white copy of photo with white border. Print color copy of same photo. Cut section from colored photo and affix directly over black-and-white image with foam adhesive.

Jennifer Cupp, Rock Island, Illinois

Supplies: Pink and black textured cardstocks (Bazzill); heart plaque (Making Memories); gingham ribbon; foam adhesive

Every good love story throughout time ends the same way...with a song and a prayer and faith that this special emotion gifted to humans by God and shared between partners is for today and tomorrow and eternity...

Amen

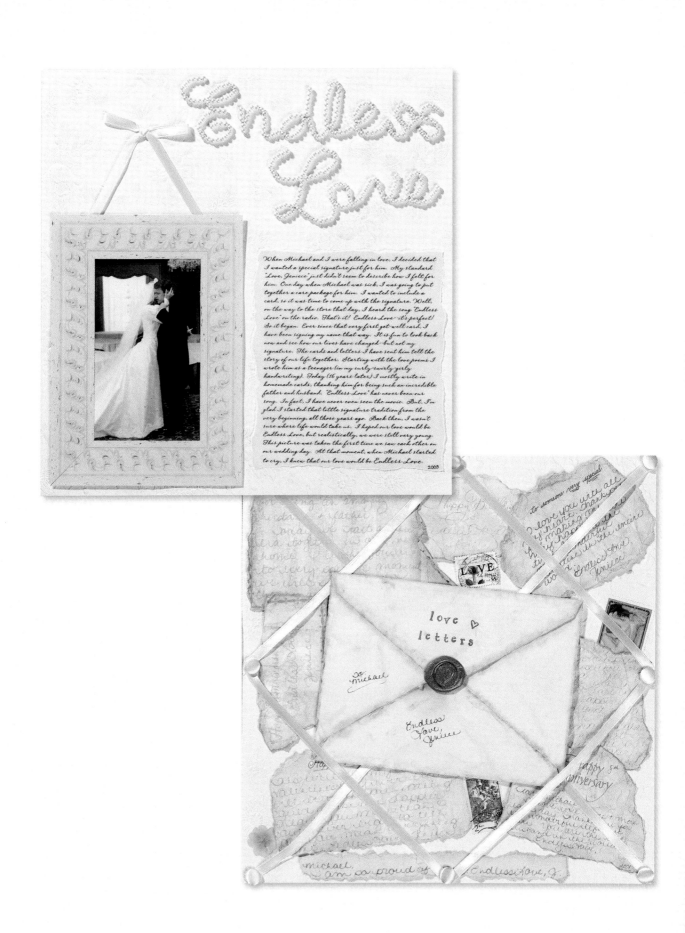

When Michael and I were falling in love, I decided that I wanted a special signature just for him. My standard "Love, Jeniece" just didn't seem to describe how I felt for him. One day when Michael was sick, I was going to put together a care package for him. I wanted to include a card, so it was time to come up with the signature. Well, on the way to the store that day, I heard the song "Endless Love" on the radio. That's it! Endless Love--it's perfect! So it began. Ever since that very first get-well card, I have been signing my name that way. It is fun to look back now and see how our lives have changed--but not my signature. The cards and letters I have sent him tell the story of our life together. Starting with the love poems I wrote him as a teenager (in my curly-swirly-girly handwriting). Today (16 years later) I mostly write in homemade cards, thanking him for being such an incredible father and husband. "Endless Love" has never been our song. In fact, I have never even seen the movie. But, I'm glad I started that little signature tradition from the very beginning, all those years ago. Back then, I wasn't sure where life would take us. I hoped our love would be Endless Love, but realistically, we were still very young. This picture was taken the first time we saw each other on our wedding day. At that moment, when Michael started to cry, I knew that our love would be Endless Love.

2000

Memorabilia is often as important as photos or journaling on a scrapbook page. It gives the page *dimension* and *texture*, providing at the same time, the perfect safe environment for storing and preserving *mementos.* Keep memorabilia away from direct contact with photos to prevent injury to your pictures. Envelopes and other PVC-free memorabilia holders offer terrific options for displaying those items most important to your *love story.*

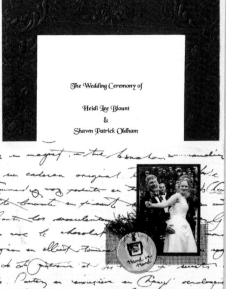

The Oldhams

A pocket holds a precious wedding program as part of this two-page spread. Begin with two cream cardstock backgrounds. On left page, ink edges of script patterned paper and mount on page. Affix mesh vertically on page; attach inked strip of patterned paper near bottom of page with brads. Mat photo on black textured cardstock; mount. Cut title from black cardstock; mount vertically on page. Stamp date on bottom left corner. On right page, mount trimmed sheet of black embossed paper onto background page. Adhere bottom and side edges of inked patterned paper to create pocket. Adorn pocket with mesh and small matted photo. Cut tiny square hole from vellum metal-rimmed tag; emboss edges of hole and tie with fiber. Adhere small photo on back and mount on mesh. Slip ceremony program in pocket.

Brandy Logan, Hendersonville, North Carolina

Supplies: Mesh (Magenta); script patterned paper (7 Gypsies); black textured cardstock (Bazzill); black embossed paper (K & Company); black embossing powder; cream cardstock; sienna ink; brad; metal-rimmed tag; fiber; date stamp

One Moment

A wedding invitation is beautifully displayed on this simple but effective page. Begin by trimming white cardstock; wrap with silk and sheer ribbons and mat on pink cardstock background page. Double and single mat photo and invitation with pink cardstock and silver paper; mount. Cut title from burgundy cardstock and mount. Embellish page with bow and title letter charms.

Sherri Brady, Victoria, British Columbia, Canada

Supplies: White, pink and burgundy cardstocks; silver paper (source unknown); title letter charms (Making Memories); silk and sheer ribbons; vellum

Unaltered By Time

A grandmother's wedding announcement and ribbon from her actual wedding bouquet are the priceless keepsakes that make this page special. Mount trimmed patterned paper piece on ivory cardstock background. Wrap opposite corners of photos with ribbon; mat on torn gold paper and mount. For frame and heart, affix torn scraps of patterned papers and cardstocks randomly on cardstock piece. Tear out rectangle block for frame; cut large "X" into rectangle and fold back flaps before mounting over photo. Attach flaps onto page with beribboned eyelets. Wrap ribbon with gold embossed charm around torn paper heart; embellish with ring before mounting. Print title on torn vellum; mount. Print copy of wedding announcement on ivory cardstock; fold and adhere patterned paper on inside. Use clear extra thick embossing enamel to cover front; cool and bend to crack and mount. Journal on torn cardstock; chalk and mount inside.

Jeanne McKinney, Huntersville, North Carolina

Supplies: Patterned papers (K & Company, Karen Foster Design, 7 Gypsies); gold paper (Bazzill); ribbon charm (Making Memories); ring charm (Boutique Trims); extra thick embossing enamel; gold embossing powder; ivory and rose cardstocks; eyelets; ribbon; vellum

Eternal Love

A painted envelope and pocket hold precious heritage photos and journaling on this historical page. Mount section of patterned paper on right side and inked section of tan cardstock on left side of black cardstock background. Triple mat photo on inked tan and black cardstocks; embellish with spiral clip and mount on page. Ink piece of patterned paper; mount on page left adhering sides and bottom only to form journaling pocket. Journal on tan cardstock and slip piece into pocket. Embellish black envelope with gingham ribbon and key charm. Adhere brads onto envelope over circle clip to create latch. Insert photos and mount. Apply rub-on title.

Angela Marvel, Puyallup, Washington

Supplies: Patterned paper (Carolee's Creations); spiral clips (7 Gypsies); rub-on words (Making Memories); key charm (source unknown); black and tan cardstocks; black ink; black envelope; gingham ribbon; brads

Something Old, Something New

Important items from this bride's wedding and extensive storytelling bring emotion to this page. Mat gray textured cardstock section at top edge of white cardstock background. Mount trimmed and torn patterned paper on white textured cardstock background, overlapping gray textured cardstock section. Create "something" title with rub-on letters. Stamp words around exposed edge of white background. Mat photo on white textured cardstock; mount and apply name with rub-on letters. Mat small photos on black cardstock. Journal on gray cardstock allowing room for matted photos and mount on white textured cardstock; affix photos and mount all on page. Add garter, earrings, stem from bouquet and pins on page. Use rub-on letters on white textured cardstock to label photos; mount under label holders.

Holly VanDyne, Mansfield, Ohio
Photos: Tim LeMasters of Keepsake Photography, Mansfield, Ohio

Supplies: White and gray textured cardstocks (Bazzill); patterned paper (KI Memories); rub-on letters (Making Memories); letter stamps (PSX Design): silver ink; black and gray cardstocks; label holders

Something Old

Something old and something blue are added to this brand-new layout. Tear edges from black cardstock; crumple and flatten. Mount on pink cardstock background; adhere handkerchief on page. Double mat photo on torn white and pink cardstocks. Roll edges of torn mat and enhance rolls with metallic rub-ons; mount on page. Set metal heart eyelets in white mat. Journal on white cardstock, framing key words; tear, roll and enhance with metallic rub-ons before mounting on page. Write descriptive words on vellum metal-rimmed tags with embossing pen; sprinkle with silver embossing powder and heat to set. Tie tags with threads and mount with heart buttons. String beads and adhere on handkerchief. Attach blue thread on page with safety pin.

Sue Schneider, Farmington, Connecticut

Supplies: Metal heart eyelets (Making Memories); metallic rub-ons (Craf-T); embossing pen (EK Success); heart buttons (Jesse James); silver embossing powder; black, pink and white cardstocks; handkerchief; metal-rimmed vellum tags; threads; beads; safety pin; blue thread

Something Old, Borrowed, Blue

A box-style layout showcases wedding memorabilia. To create windows follow directions below. Adhere elements inside openings. Attach decorative brads on corners of foam core. Ink edges of openings with red ink. Use letter stickers to apply title. Embellish page with metal word plaques, pewter heart, tassel, ribbon trim above garter belt, and wedding plaque rubbed with pigment powders.

Colleen Macdonald, Winthrop, Australia

Supplies: Patterned paper (source unknown); handmade paper (source unknown); decorative brads (Making Memories); letter stickers (Li'l Davis Designs, Provo Craft, Me & My Big Ideas, Wordsworth); metal word plaques (Li'l Davis Designs); pewter heart (Magenta); wedding plaque (Darice); pigment powders (AMACO); serrated foam core; red cardstock; red ink; tassel; ribbon trim

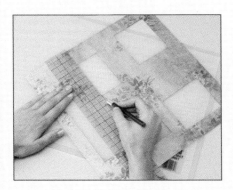

1 Cut window openings from a sheet of patterned paper.

2 Place cut piece of patterned paper over a serrated sheet of foam core. Mark window openings on foam core and cut. Adhere cut patterned paper to cut foam core.

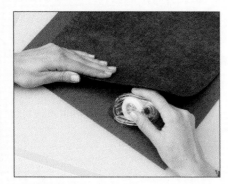

3 Mount a sheet of mulberry paper in the center of a red cardstock background. Adhere foam core section atop background allowing mulberry to show through window opening.

Full of Promise

Countless hours spent sewing a wedding dress are journaled on this page, as perfect as that gown. Begin by adhering silk ribbon along edges of black cardstock background; add bows in corners. Trim black cardstock piece slightly smaller than ribbon borders; cover with lace fabric, embellish with pearl buttons; mount on background with foam adhesive. Mount "Full of Promise" preprinted transparency on white handmade paper and adhere vertically on page. Journal on transparency strip and affix on title block; embellish edges with pearl strands. Cut preprinted "of life...of love..." transparency to fit photo; attach onto photo with brads and mount. Cut a variety of tags from handmade paper including two for a shaker box. Embellish with silk flower, letter stickers, photo and gold-beaded trim. Create shaker box by cutting window from a tag; adhere scrap of page protector behind window opening. Lay beads and marbles on second tag and mount the two tags together with foam adhesive. Mount all tags on page over strands of pearls and ribbon and embellish with pearl straight pins.

Colleen Macdonald, Winthrop, Australia

Supplies: Pearl/gemstone buttons (Elan/H.A. Kidd and Co.); preprinted transparency (Artistic Expressions); white handmade paper and tag template (Provo Craft); letter stickers (Wordsworth); silk ribbon; bows; black cardstock; lace fabric; pearl strand; brads; gold beaded trim; pearl straight pins; marbles; page protector scrap; foam adhesive

White Lace & Promises

Hidden journaling explains the significance of this layout's title on a crystal-beaded page. Cut window openings for memorabilia in foam core board. Cut windows out of fabric paper and adhere on top of foam core. Attach back of foam core to cardstock; mount rice bag and garter in openings. Affix crystal-beaded trim across top of board; add blue fabric paper strip. Mount title printed on vellum across strip. Double mat photos on blue fabric paper and pieces cut from fabric wallpaper; mount on page leaving left side of horizontal photo free to allow journaling tag to slip behind. Journal on fabric wallpaper piece; attach heart brad and slip behind photo.

Jenny Moore Lowe, Lafayette, Colorado
Photos: Owens Photography

Supplies: Blue fabric paper (K & Company); beaded trim (The Berry Patch); foam core board; rice bag; garter belt; vellum; fabric wallpaper; heart brad

Program

A story behind the wedding programs that almost didn't happen and the program itself make this page unique. Begin by adhering small and large blocks of green patterned paper on burgundy patterned paper background. Mat focal photo on black cardstock and mount. Embellish smaller patterned paper piece with die-cut heart, printed ribbon and gold-leafed metal heart. Create pocket for program by cutting a double frame from green and brown patterned papers. Mount quote printed on vellum behind frame and over photo. Attach brads and mount on page with foam adhesive to form pocket; insert program. Journal on cream cardstock leaving room for photo; chalk edges and mount on page with photo and printed ribbon. Embellish ribbon with gold-leafed metal heart. Cut title from black cardstock; mount above journaling.

Michelle Pesce, Arvada, Colorado
Photos: Eliot Khuner Photography, Berkeley, California

Supplies: Green and burgundy patterned papers, metal hearts, printed ribbon (Making Memories, Mustard Moon); die-cut heart (Sizzix); gold leafing pen (Krylon); black and cream cardstocks; brads; foam adhesive; chalk

Mementos From Our Wedding

Exhaustive journaling and a frilly hankie tell a memorable story on this page. Journal on beige cardstock leaving spaces for various objects; trim and mount on tan cardstock background. Adhere thin border strips cut from tan cardstock on each side of journaling box; embellish with tan trim. Adhere strips of brown cardstock on both sides of tan strips. Print title information on vellum; sprinkle with white embossing powder and heat to set. Ink backside with brown ink; mount. Using computer software, apply word on photo; tear and mount on page. Frame small photo with brass frame and mount. Stitch handkerchief together adorning with ring; stitch to page.

Samantha Walker, Battle Ground, Washington
Photo: Mark Philbrick Photography, Orem, Utah

Supplies: Brass frame (Fancy Buckle Series); beige, tan and brown cardstocks; white embossing powder; tan trim; vellum; brown ink

Additional Art/Credits

United (Cover)

Attach pearl beads to edges of pearl metallic background paper by stitching in place. Dampen, crumple and flatten cream metallic paper; when dry cut and stitch to background. Mat photos on white pearl paper; ink mat edges gold. Sew beaded sections to edge of smaller photo mat. Mat larger photo on gold metallic paper; crop and punch edges before mounting photo on mat and again on background. Wrap wide ribbon vertically at right side of page; secure. Tie small ribbon around center of wider ribbon; embellish with satin leaves, paper flowers, sprigs, sprays and rings. Write title and journal on vellum and gold emboss; heat set. Crop, ink edges and mount to page. Add remaining page embellishments.

Jodi Amidei, Memory Makers Books
Photos: Christina Slater, Denver, Colorado

Supplies: Metallic papers (Paper Adventures); pearl beads, paper roses (Westrim); decorative corner punch (EK Success); pearl sprigs and sprays, satin leaves (Everlasting Elegance); gold rings (Darice); gold embossing powder; gold ink; wide satin ribbon; small silk ribbon

Wedding Bookplate (Pg. 3)

Trim patterned paper to desired size; cover with embossed vellum cut to fit. Enhance embossed vellum with gold pigment powder; adhere flower stickers. Emboss all edges in gold embossing powder. Affix lace trim along top, adding gold beads as shown. Affix pearl string along sides and bottom adding gold beads on bottom corners. Pull length of tulle through large beads; adhere on top corners of piece.

Torrey Miller, Thornton, Colorado

Supplies: Patterned paper (K & Company); embossed vellum (Paper Adventures); pigment powder (Jacquard); flower stickers (EK Success); beads and pearl string (Westrim); gold embossing powder; lace trim; tulle

Dreams Come True (Pg. 6)

Adhere torn strips of patterned paper on purple textured cardstock background. Mount photo on page. Journal on vellum and mount on page near photo. Frame photo in purple satin ribbon, embellishing corners with small silk flowers. Handcut title words and mount on page and behind clear plastic tag. Stamp small heart design on tag; tie ribbon and mount tag to page. Embellish with strung pearl border.

Supplies: Patterned paper (K & Company); purple textured cardstock (Bazzill); tag (Creek Bank Creations); silk flowers; ink; strung pearl border

A Wedding (Pg. 12)

Begin with green textured cardstock background; tear section from floral patterned paper and mount vertically on page. Print title and poem on top of vellum piece torn to fit floral patterned paper piece; punch squares from bottom and mount over floral section. Mat photos on red textured cardstock; mount on page.

Lori Dickhaut, Sherwood Park, Alberta, Canada

Supplies: Floral patterned paper (Masterpiece Studios); green and red textured cardstocks (DMD); square punches (Marvy); clear vellum

I Never Dreamed (Pg. 12)

Begin by mounting section cut from floral patterned paper across top of green textured cardstock background. Print title and poem on right side of clear vellum cut to fit patterned paper piece; mount on top of it. Mat photos on red and yellow textured cardstocks; adhere on page.

Lori Dickhaut, Sherwood Park, Alberta, Canada

Supplies: Floral patterned paper (Masterpiece Studios); green, yellow, and red textured cardstock (DMD); clear vellum

Beauty of a Bride (Pg. 12)

Tear corner sections of floral papttterned paper; mount in opposite corners of two textured green cardstock background pages. Mat four photos on red and yellow cardstock; mount on background pages. Mount unmatted photo on right page. Journal on vellum; tear and mount over photos and torn patterned paper corner sections.

Lori Dickhaut, Sherwood Park, Alberta, Canada

Supplies: Textured cardstock (DMD); patterned paper (Masterpiece Studios); vellum; poem (internet, author unknown)

With This Ring (Pg. 13)

Begin with two green textured cardstock backgrounds; mount cut sections vertically on both pages as shown. Cut clear vellum sections to fit patterned paper sections; print title on one and poem on other and adhere both on pages. Affix fuzzy fiber along edge of title bar and on both sides of poem. Mat photos for left page on a single sheet of yellow cardstock; mount on page. Mat photo for right page on red textured cardstock; mount on page. Punch squares from patterned paper; mat on red cardstock and adhere on right page.

Lori Dickhaut, Sherwood Park, Alberta, Canada

Supplies: Floral patterned paper (Masterpiece Studios); square punches (Marvy); green and red textured cardstock (DMD); yellow cardstock; clear vellum; fuzzy fibers

Signature (Pg. 13)

Lori documents the signing of the marriage papers with a bright, light layout. Begin with two green textured cardstock backgrounds; mount cut sections of floral patterned paper vertically on left page, and horizontally on right page. Print title and poem on bottom of one of two sheets of clear vellum cut to fit patterned paper sections. Wrap fiber around title sheet; mount both sheets atop patterned paper pieces. Mat photos on yellow and red textured cardstocks; mount on page. Cut tag from red textured cardstock; set eyelet in top and tie with silk ribbon. Decorate tag by layering torn patterned paper and vellum; wrap with various fibers and ribbon and mount on upper right corner of right page.

Lori Dickhaut, Sherwood Park, Alberta, Canada

Supplies: Floral patterned paper (Masterpiece Studios); green and red textured cardstock (DMD); yellow cardstock; clear vellum; fibers; silk ribbon; eyelet

In the Sand (Pg. 13)

Lori re-creates the elements in the photos with various patterned papers and brightly colored cardstocks. Layer torn sections of sand patterned paper and floral patterned paper on two green textured cardstock backgrounds. Print title and poem on top right corner of clear vellum; tear and mount on left page. Tear bottom right corner of vellum sheet; mount on right page. Mat photos on red and yellow textured cardstock; adhere on both pages.

Lori Dickhaut, Sherwood Park, Alberta, Canada

Supplies: Sand patterned paper (Wübie); floral patterned paper (Masterpiece Studios); green, red, and yellow textured cardstocks (DMD); clear vellum

Will You Marry Me? (Pg. 14)

Wrap sheer burgundy ribbon horizontally across upper and lower portions of patterned paper background. Mount patterned paper on black cardstock. Tear strip of patterned paper and ink and emboss edges; mount on lower sheer ribbon. Mount second piece of decorated ribbon on top of torn strip; embellish with beads. Mat photos on black cardstock; wrap photo corners of primary photo with sheer ribbon and mount all photos on background. Stamp "Will you?" title on pink vellum; cut into oval and mount under embossed gold metal tag; embellish with silk flowers. Journal remaining title and journaling portion and cut into strips. Mount "marry me?" over photo and place remaining strips in organza bag; mount on page.

Jodi Amidei, Memory Makers Books
Photos: Bruce Aldridge, Broomfield, Colorado

Supplies: Patterned paper (Sandylion); vellum (Autumn Leaves); metal tag (Making Memories); stamps (Technique Tuesday); ribbon, organza ribbon, organza bag, beads, ink, embossing powder

First Baptist Church (Pg. 26)

Trim and mat embossed paper on black textured cardstock background. Paint ribbon charm; when dry, slip velvet ribbon through and mount vertically on page. Double mat photo on cream and black cardstock; adhere with foam adhesive. Print title on cream cardstock; cut out and enhance with metallic rub-ons. Mat on black cardstock wrapping ends with velvet ribbon and attaching painted decorative brads. Adhere with foam tape on page. For stained-glass piece, paint transparency pieces in jewel tones; sprinkle with clear embossing powder and heat to set. Repeat this for date piece. Adhere pieces and date on separate transparency sheet and mount on page. Adhere another sheet atop piece with foam adhesive. Draw "grout" lines on top transparency with permanent marker. Adorn page with large painted ribbon charm strung with velvet ribbon.

Denise Tucker, Versailles, Indiana
Photo: Robert Huddle Photography, Galesburg, Illinois

Supplies: Embossed paper (Paper Adventures); black textured cardstock (Bazzill); ribbon charms, decorative brads (Making Memories); metallic rub-ons (Craf-T); clear embossing powder; permanent marker (Sanford); cream and black cardstocks; velvet ribbon; paints; transparencies

Endless Love (Pg. 116)

Jeniece tells the story of how she came up with the special signature she made up just for her husband and uses her two-page spread to document it. Begin with two cream embossed cardstock backgrounds. On left page, frame photo with paper frame; mount on page using foam adhesive and ribbon. Journal on vellum; tear out and adhere on page. To make title, string beads on wire and bend to form letters; affix on page. On right page, create a memory board by scanning old letters or memorabilia; tear out sections, chalk to age, and adhere on background page with stamps and pressed flower. Cover page in a crisscross pattern with silk ribbon; attach silk buttons as shown. Age envelope and stamp the contents on top flap. Place wax disk on corner of flap; heat until soft and press with seal. Use envelope to hold memorabilia.

Jeniece Higgins, Lake Forest, Illinois

Supplies: Cream embossed cardstock (K & Company); paper frame (My Mind's Eye); letter stamps and heart stamp (Hero Arts); wax disk; seal; pressed flower; vellum; ribbon; wire; beads; chalk; postage stamps; silk ribbon; silk ribbon; envelope

Backgrounds

Pages 1-13 and 124-128, (Making Memories)
Pages 14-25, (KI Memories)
Pages 26-115 (Ever After Paper Company)
Pages 116-124 (Making Memories)

Sources

The following companies manufacture products showcased on scrapbook pages within this book. Please check your local retailers to find these materials. We have made every attempt to properly credit the items mentioned in this book and apologize to those we may have missed.

3L Corporation
(800) 828-3130
www.scrapbook-adhesives.com

3M
(800) 364-3577
www.3m.com

7 Gypsies
(800) 588-6707
www.7gypsies.com

AC Moore—no contact info available

Accu-Cut® (wholesale only)
(800) 288-1670
www.accucut.com

Adobe
www.adobe.com

All My Memories
(888) 553-1998
www.allmymemories.com

All Night Media (see Plaid Enterprises)

All The Extras- no longer in business

American Art Clay Company (AMACO)
(800) 374-1600
www.amaco.com

Amscan, Inc.
(800) 444-8887
www.amscan.com

Anna Griffin, Inc (wholesale only)
(888) 817-8170
www.annagriffin.com

Arbee Crafts—no contact info available

Arches—no contact info available

ARTChix Studio
(250) 370-9885
www.artchixstudio.com

Artistic Expressions
(219) 764-5158
www.artisticexpressionsinc.com

Artistic Scrapper
(818) 786-8304
www.artisticscrapper.com

Autumn Leaves (wholesale only)
(800) 588-6707
www.autumnleaves.com

Avery Dennison Corporation
(800) GO-AVERY
www.avery.com

Bazzill Basics Paper
(480) 558-8557
www.bazzillbasics.com

Berry Patch, The—no contact info available

Biblical Impressions
(877) 587-0941
www.biblical.com

Blumenthal Lansing
(201) 935-6220
www.buttonsplus.com

Bo-Bunny Press
(801) 771-0481
www.bobunny.com

Boutique Trims, Inc.
(248) 437-2017
www.boutiquetrims.com

Boxer Scrapbook Productions
(503) 625-0455
www.boxerscrapbooks.com

Broderbund Software
www.broderbund.com

Canson, Inc.®
(800) 628-9283
www.canson-us.com

Card Connection, The (see Michaels Arts & Crafts)

CARL Mfg. USA, Inc. (wholesale only)
(800) 257-4771
www.Carl-Products.com

Carole Fabrics
(706) 863-4742
www.carolefabrics.com

Carolee's Creations®
(435) 563-1100
www.carolees.com

ChartPak
(800) 628-1910
www.chartpak.com

Chatterbox, Inc.
(208) 939-9133
www.chatterboxinc.com

Clearsnap, Inc.
(800) 448-4862
www.clearsnap.com

Close To My Heart®
(888) 655-6552
www.closetomyheart.com

Cloud 9 Design
(763) 493-0990
www.cloud9design.biz

Club Scrap™
(888) 634-9100
www.clubscrap.com

Colorbök™, Inc. (wholesale only)
(800) 366-4660
www.colorbok.com

Craf-T Products
(507) 235-3996
www.craf-tproducts.com

Crafter's Workshop, The
(877) CRAFTER
www.thecraftersworkshop.com

Crafts, Etc. Ltd.
(800) 888-0321
www.craftsetc.com

Creative Imaginations (wholesale only)
(800) 942-6487
www.cigift.com

Creative Impressions
(719) 596-4860
www.creativeimpressions.com

Creek Bank Creations, Inc.
(217) 427-5980
www.creekbankcreations.com

Cropper Hopper™/Advantus Corporation (wholesale only)
(800) 826-8806
www.cropperhopper.com

C-Thru® Ruler Company, The (wholesale only)
(800) 243-8419
www.cthruruler.com

Current®, Inc.
(800) 848-2848
www.currentinc.com

Daisy D's Paper Company
(888) 601-8955
www.daisydspaper.com

Daisy Hill—no contact info available

Daler-Rowney USA
(609) 655-5252
www.daler-rowney.com

Darice, Inc.
(800) 321-1494
www.darice.com

DecoArt™, Inc.
(800) 367-3047
www.decoart.com

Delta Technical Coatings, Inc.
(800) 423-4135
www.deltacrafts.com

Deluxe Designs
(480) 497-9005
www.deluxecuts.com

Design Originals
(800) 877-7820
www.d-originals.com

DieCuts with a View™
(801) 224-6766
www.diecutswithaview.com

DMD Industries, Inc. (wholesale only)
(800) 805-9890
www.dmdind.com

Dreamweaver Stencils
(909) 824-8343
www.dreamweaverstencils.com

Duncan Enterprises
(800) 782-6748
www.duncan-enterprises.com

Dymo
www.dymo.com

Eggery Place, The
www.theeggeryplace.com

EK Success™, Ltd. (wholesale only)
(800) 524-1349
www.eksuccess.com

Elan/H.A. Kidd and Company—no contact info available

Emagination Crafts, Inc. (wholesale only)
(630) 833-9521
www.emaginationcrafts.com

Everlasting Elegance—no contact info available

Fancy Buckle Series—no contact info available

Fiskars, Inc. (wholesale only)
(715) 842-2091
www.fiskars.com

FLAX art & design
(415) 330-3208
www.flaxart.com

Foofala
(402) 330-3208
www.foofala.com

Frances Meyer, Inc.®
(800) 372-6237
www.francesmeyer.com

Funk and Wagnall's—no contact info available

Gifted Line, The
(800) 533-7263

Graffitti—no contact info available

Graphic Products Corporation
(800) 323-1660
www.gpcpapers.com

Halcraft USA, Inc.
(212) 376-1580
www.halcraft.com

Hambly Studios, Inc.
(800) 451-3999
www.hamblystudios.com

Hero Arts® Rubber Stamps, Inc. (wholesale only)
(800) 822-4376
www.heroarts.com

Hirschberg, Schutz & Co., Inc.
(800) 221-8640

Hobby Lobby Stores, Inc.
www.hobbylobby.com

Hot Off The Press, Inc.
(800) 227-9595
www.paperpizazz.com

Impress Rubber Stamps
(206) 901-9101
www.impressrubberstamps.com

Inkadinkado® Rubber Stamps
(800) 888-4652
www.inkadinkado.com

It Takes Two®
(800) 331-9843
www.ittakestwo.com

Jacquard Products/Rupert, Gibbon & Spider, Inc.
(800) 442-0455
www.jacquardproducts.com

Jasc Software
(800) 622-2793
www.jasc.com

JBW—no contact info available

Jennifer Collection, The
(518) 272-4572
www.paperdiva.net

Jesse James & Co., Inc.
(610) 435-0201
www.jessejamesbutton.com

Jest Charming
(702) 564-5101
www.jestcharming.com

Jo-Ann Fabrics & Crafts
(888) 739-4120
www.joann.com

JudiKins
(310) 515-1115
www.judikins.com

Junkitz™
(212) 944-4250
www.junkitz.com

K & Company
(888) 244-2083
www.kandcompany.com

Karen Foster Design™ (wholesale only)
(801) 451-9779
www.karenfosterdesign.com

KI Memories
www.kimemories.com

Kopp Design
(208) 656-0734
www.koppdesign.com

Krylon
(216) 566-2000
www.krylon.com

La Pluma, Inc.
(615) 273-7367
www.debrabeagle.com

Li'l Davis Designs
(949) 838-0344
www.lildavisdesigns.com

Liquitex® Artist Materials
(888) 4-ACRYLIC
www.liquitex.com

Magenta Rubber Stamps (wholesale only)
(800) 565-5254
www.magentarubberstamps.com

Magic Mesh™
(651) 345-6374
www.magicmesh.com

Magic Scraps™
(972) 238-1838
www.magicscraps.com

Making Memories
(800) 286-5263
www.makingmemories.com

Mark Richards Enterprises, Inc.
(888) 901-0091
www.markrichardsusa.com

Marvy® Uchida (wholesale only)
(800) 541-5877
www.uchida.com

Masterpiece® Studios
(800) 447-0219
www.masterpiecestudios.com

Ma Vinci's Reliquary
http://crafts.dm.net/mall//reliquary

me & my BiG ideas® (wholesale only)
(949) 583-2065
www.meandmybigideas.com

Memories Complete™, LLC
(866) 966-6365
www.memoriescomplete.com

Memory Lane—no contact info available

Michaels® Arts & Crafts
(800) 642-4235
www.michaels.com

Microsoft Corporation
www.microsoft.com

Mrs. Grossman's Paper Co.
(wholesale only)
(800) 429-4549
www.mrsgrossmans.com

Mustard Moon™
(408) 229-8542
www.mustardmoon.com

My Mind's Eye™, Inc.
(801) 298-3709
www.frame-ups.com

Nancy Phelps—no contact info available

National Artcraft Co.
(888) 937-2723
www.nationalartcraft.com

Natural Paper Co., The—no contact info available

Nature's Handmade Paper, LLC
(800) 861-7050
www.natureshandmadepaper.com

NRN Designs
(800) 421-6958
www.nrndesigns.com

Nunn Design
(360) 379-3557
www.nunndesign.com

Offray
www.offray.com

Paper Adventures® (wholesale only)
(800) 727-0699
www.paperadventures.com

Paper Cut—no contact info available

Paper House Productions
(800) 255-7316
www.paperhouseproductions.com

Paper Loft, The
(801) 254-1961
www.paperloft.com

Pebbles, Inc.
(800) 438-8153
www.pebblesinc.com

Penny Black Inc.
(510) 849-1883
www.pennyblackinc.com

Pioneer Photo Albums, Inc.®
(800) 366-3686
www.pioneerphotoalbums.com

Plaid Enterprises, Inc.
(800) 842-4197
www.plaidonline.com

Pressed Petals
(800) 748-4656
www.pressedpetals.com

Prickley Pear Rubber Stamps
www.prickleypear.com

PrintWorks
(800) 854-6558
www.printworkscollection.com

Provo Craft® (wholesale only)
(888) 577-3545
www.provocraft.com

Prym-Dritz Corporation
www.dritz.com

PSX Design™
(800) 782-6748
www.psxdesign.com

Pulsar Paper Products
(877) 861-0031
www.pulsarpaper.com

Quest Beads & Cast, Inc.
(212) 354-0979
www.questbeads.com

QuicKutz®
(888) 702-1146
www.quickutz.com

Ranger Industries, Inc.
(800) 244-2211
www.rangerink.com

Razzle Dazzle—no contact info available

Reena's Creations—no contact info available

Robert's Crafts—no contact info available

Rubber Baby Buggy Bumpers
(970) 224-3499
www.rubberbaby.com

Rubber Stampede
(800) 423-4135
www.rubberstampede.com

Rusty Pickle
(801) 272-2280
www.rustypickle.com

Sakura Hobby Craft
(310) 212-7878
www.sakuracraft.com

Sanford® Corp.
(800) 323-0749
www.sanfordcorp.com

Santa Rosa—no contact info available

Sarah Heidt Photo Craft
(734) 424-2776
www.SarahHeidtPhotoCraft.com

Scrap Ease®
(800) 272-3874
www.whatsnewltd.com

Scrap Pagerz™
(435) 645-0696
www.scrappagerz.com

Scrapbook Mania
(318) 636-7601
www.scrapbookmaniac.com

Scrapworks, LLC
(801) 363-1010
www.scrapworks.com

Serendipity Paper
www.serendipitypaper.com

Sizzix
(866) 742-4447
www.sizzix.com

Southworth Company
(800) 225-1839
www.southworth.com

S.R.M. Press, Inc.
(800) 323-9589
www.srmpress.com

Stampabilities
(800) 888-0321
www.stampabilities.com

Stampers Anonymous/The Creative Block
(888) 326-0012
www.stampersanonymous.com

Stampin' Up!®
(800) 782-6787
www.stampinup.com

StenSource® International, Inc.
(800) 642-9293
www.stensource.com

Sunshine Papers
(435) 628-2528
www.sunshinepapers.com

Target
www.target.com

Treehouse Designs
(877) 372-1109
www.treehouse-designs.com

Tsukineko®, Inc.
(800) 769-6633
www.tsukineko.com

USArtQuest
(800) 200-7848
www.usartquest.com

Wal-Mart Stores, Inc.
(800) WALMART
www.walmart.com

Wasau Papers—no contact info available

Waterman—no contact info available

Westrim® Crafts
(800) 727-2727
www.westrimcrafts.com

Willow Bead—no contact info available

Wilton Enterprises
(630) 810-2205
www.wilton.com

Windsor Newton Gallery—no contact info available

Wintech International Corp.
(800) 263-6043
www.wintechint.com

Woodland Scenics
(573) 346-5555
www.woodlandscenics.com

Wordsworth
(719) 282-3495
www.wordsworthstamps.com

Wübie Prints
(888) 256-0107
www.wubieprints.com

Index